Happy Co

RELISH
YORKSHIRE

Original recipes from the region's finest chefs

First Published 2009
By Relish Publications
Shield Green Farm, Tritlington,
Northumberland NE61 3DX

ISBN 978-0-9564205-0-3

Editor: Duncan Peters
Design: Euan Underwood, room501 publishing
Photography: NR Photography, Tony May Images
(1885 The Restaurant)

Printed by Europa PO Box 6070, Cardiff, CF15 9AU

RELISH
PUBLICATIONS.CO.UK

004
CONTENTS

STARTERS

MAINS

DESSERTS

RESTAURANT

INTRODUCTION WITH ROSEMARY SHRAGER

I love living in Yorkshire, and I am so proud to take part in the life of the culinary world of a county where we truly have the best of everything at our disposal. As the largest county in Great Britain, with four million acres, Yorkshire boasts an amazing range of produce of wonderful quality and diversity. These rich soils and the practice of good strong husbandry, following traditional methods with animals reared naturally in the outdoors on grassland and the moors, is the standard by which we get food tasting as it should. One common factor in cooking is that the ingredients come first. Cooking in season is easy and here we know when farmers and food producers will be harvesting locally, so we can enjoy produce when it is naturally at its best, then when the season finishes look forward to the next year. Supermarkets can be quite confusing when they produce all the year round.

Our restaurants and hotels are some of the country's best and we have many terrific award winning restaurants here, all with very talented and passionate chefs. Simon Gueller, Simon Crannage, Harvey Nicks, the Devonshire Arms are just some of those who contribute greatly to the strength of Yorkshire's reputation as a great place for exceptional food. Yorkshire chefs are very good at sourcing local produce; it helps the chef to write and describe his menus. From our marvellous fishing ports down the coast from Whitby to Hull, to our Hill lamb, to our Dales creameries and Huddersfield curd cheese, our produce is sought by discerning food fans all over the country, and of course it doesn't stop there. I really am very proud to have Yorkshire blood in me, and proud to be associated with a book that champions everything that this wonderful area has to offer.

Rosemary Shrager
TV celebrity chef Rosemary starred in ITV's Ladettes to Ladies and Rosemary Shrager's School for Cooks. She also runs a very successful cookery school at Swinton Park Hotel – see page 128 for details.

008
1885 THE RESTAURANT

The Recreation Ground, Stainland, Halifax, West Yorkshire HX4 9HF

01422 373 030
www.1885therestaurant.co.uk

"Overlooking the idyllic Pennine hills, 1885 The Restaurant lies in elegant seclusion amidst its rustic surroundings. The family run restaurant is sophisticated but unassuming, with a relaxed and informal ambience, a warm and personal service, and consistently fabulous food. Proprietors and chefs Nathan and Matthew Evans are local lads who's cooking skills are regarded by many as the best in these parts. They have spread their wings far and wide to learn the culinary craft working and dining in some of the best restaurants in the country, before returning to their home village and making a big impact on the Yorkshire dining scene. Great pride is taken in sourcing the very best fresh seasonal ingredients to create menus buzzing with bold ideas, with dishes elegantly presented and precisely balanced in texture and taste. The resulting cuisine finds equilibrium in an amalgamation of the modern and the traditional, the English and the continental, the basic and the intricate.

These ambitious and committed young chefs are making quite a name for themselves, and challenging the longer-established restaurants in the region to raise their game lest they get left behind."

Jamie Rhodes,
Author and Critic

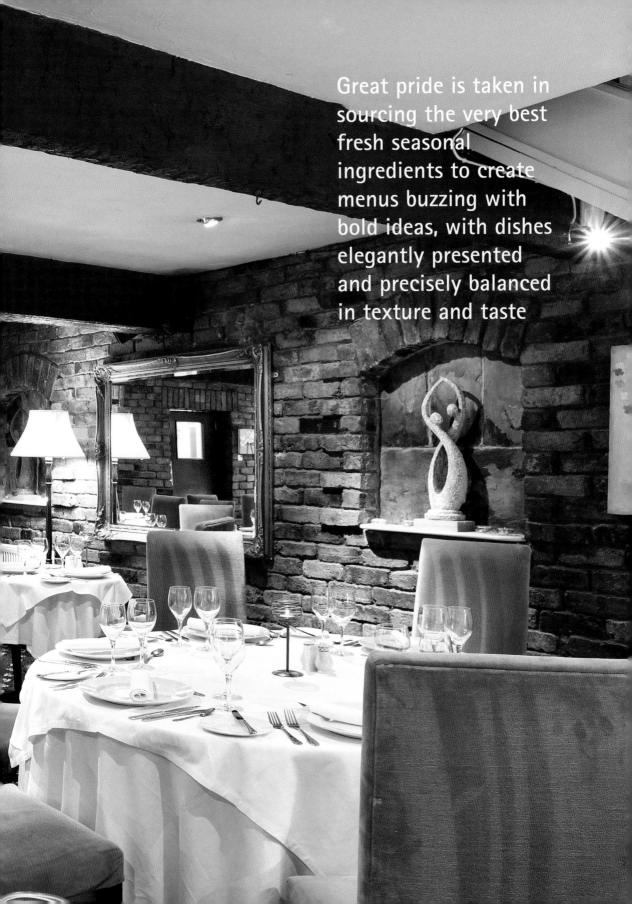

Great pride is taken in sourcing the very best fresh seasonal ingredients to create menus buzzing with bold ideas, with dishes elegantly presented and precisely balanced in texture and taste

POACHED SALMON
RADISH, CUCUMBER, LIME
SERVES 8

Ingredients

1 side salmon, skinned and pin boned
8 large radishes, thinly sliced
1 cucumber
2 limes, segmented and juice kept
6 leaves bronze gelatine, soaked in cold water
250ml stock syrup

Court bouillon

1 litre fish stock
1 carrot peeled
1 celery peeled
1 shallot peeled
1 fennel washed
3 star anise bulbs
Small bunch parsley washed
6 cloves
1 lemon

Method

For the cucumber strips

Top and tail the cucumber and with a vegetable peeler, peel the cucumber trying to keep the strips as long as possible save the inside of the cucumber for the jelly. Line the cucumber strips together on a chopping board and cut each end off to leave you with about 8cm long strips all the same size.

For the cucumber jelly

Take the peeled cucumber and cut in half long ways and juice through a vegetable juicer. This should yield about 250ml of cucumber juice. Add the stock syrup and reserved lime juice and then boil the mixture with a little sugar, then season to taste. When boiling take off the stove and add the squeezed out gelatine whisk until dissolved then pass into a rectangle tub lined out with cling film. Place in the fridge for 4 hours to set.

For the poaching the salmon

First make the court bouillon. Roughly chop up the vegetables and lemon and add them to a deep roasting tin. Place directly on the heat with the fish stock, star anise, peppercorns, parsley and cloves. Add a little salt and pepper Bring the court bouillon to the boil and turn down to a simmer about 80°c.

Meanwhile trim the salmon fillet lay the skinned salmon down service side up on a chopping board. Start by cutting the salmon into a large rectangle by trimming down the sides and topping and tailing the fish ends then cut in to 8 equal parts.

Add the salmon steaks to the roasting tin with the simmering court bouillon. Cook for 4-5 minutes if you like your salmon just cooked or 10-12 minutes if you like your salmon well done. Turn off the heat after the approximate time and leave the salmon to cool in the bouillon to absorb the flavour of the vegetables and spices.

Assembling the dish

On a long white rectangle plate start by laying 2 cucumber strips next to each other in the middle. Take a piece of salmon out of the court bouillon drain off any excess liquid. Place on top of the cucumber strips and place a segment of lime on top. Cut the cucumber jelly into 1cm squares and add 3 of them to the salmon dish, then add 3 slices of radish and some cress for garnish.

MALLARD BREAST & LEG
WATERMELON, SWEETCORN, LIQUORICE
SERVES 4

Ingredients

2 whole mallard
500g rendered duck fat
1 watermelon
4 corn on the cob
2 sticks liquorice
1 bunch baby watercress
Sea salt
2 rosemary sticks

Duck Stock

2 sticks celery chopped
1 onion chopped
2 carrots chopped
2 star anise bulbs
250g tomato purée
1 large glass red wine

Method

For the duck

First take off the mallard legs and rub with sea salt and rosemary leave to marinate overnight. Then cover the mallard legs in the duck fat and confit at 110°c for 3 hours, meanwhile take the breast off the mallard, season lightly and set to one side.

For the stock

Pre heat oven to 250°c. Roast the duck bones in an oven tray with the celery, onion, carrots, star anise and tomato purée until browned for about half an hour. Then re boil everything in a large stock pot with water to just cover the bones, reduce by half, then pass into a clean pan. Add the red wine and liquorice reduce by a third, season to taste, pass again then set to one side

For the sweetcorn purée

Start by tearing off the outer leaves of the corn then place in a pan and cover with milk, add a little sugar, salt and pepper and boil for 40/50 minutes until soft. Take the corn out of the pan and pass ½ of the milk into a clean pan, cut the corn off the cob and add back to the milk in the pan re boil. Once the corn is soft whiz to a soft purée and set aside to cool

For the watermelon

Skin the watermelon, then slice into 1cm slabs, then dice into 1cm cubes, remove seeds, fry in a little olive oil till golden brown, season lightly and set aside.

For the duck breast

Score the fat on the duck breast very finely, seal in a hot pan fat side down to render. Seal the other side then place in a hot oven for 5 minutes. Pull out of the oven and leave to rest for 10 minutes, carve and serve pink.

Assembling the dish

Re-heat each individual element for the dish, plate up on hot plates, drizzle with the liquorice sauce and garnish with baby watercress.

WHITE CHOCOLATE PAVE
DARK CHOCOLATE, WALNUT, LOLLY

SERVES 8

Ingredients

White chocolate pave

500g white chocolate, 80% cocoa solids
360ml whole milk
6 leaves bronze gelatine, soaked in cold water
50ml good quality brandy
1 vanilla pod split
250ml cream, whipped

Malted dark chocolate mousse

500g dark chocolate, 80% cocoa solids
360ml whole milk
6 leaves bronze gelatine soaked in cold water
200g Horlicks
250ml cream, whipped

Caramelised walnuts

500g whole walnuts, shelled
200g caster sugar
5tbsp water

Chocolate liqueur lolly

250ml white chocolate liqueur
250ml stock syrup
1 vanilla pod split, seeds only
2 leaves gelatine, soaked in cold water
Lolly sticks cut in half

Method

For the chocolate liqueur lolly

Take the stock syrup and bring to the boil. When boiling pull off the stove and then squeeze out the water from the gelatine and add to the hot syrup then add vanilla seeds and chocolate liqueur. Whisk to melt all the gelatine, pour into an ice cream machine and churn until nearly frozen. Spoon into ice cube moulds and freeze. After 1½ hours push a lolly stick in each of the ice cube moulds.

For the malted dark chocolate mousse

In a bowl add the chocolate and the squeezed out gelatine and set aside. Boil the whole milk and Horlicks and pour over the chocolate mixture, leave to steep for 2 minutes then whisk well. Fold in the whipped cream, pour into a tub and place in the fridge for 4 hours to set.

For the white chocolate pave

Place the white chocolate, squeezed out gelatine, vanilla seeds and brandy in a bowl, boil the milk and when boiling add to the chocolate mixture. Leave to steep for 2 minutes then whisk well. Fold in the whipped cream and pour into a long rectangle dish, about 1½ inches deep. Place in the fridge to set for about 3-4 hours.

For the caramelised walnuts

In a pan bring the caster sugar and water to the boil. Once boiling leave until a light caramel colour is achieved, then add the walnuts gently and quickly stir with a wooden spoon. Pour out onto a non stick tray and leave to cool.

Assembling the dish

At one end of a long white plate firstly place a piece of the white chocolate pave by cutting a nice pave style piece from the block. Next with an ice cream scoop (in hot water) ball the malted dark chocolate mousse and place in the middle of the plate. Then take out the ice cube moulds and pop out a mini ice cream (if they stick rub underneath with a cloth soaked in hot water until they become loose). Place at the opposite end to the white chocolate pave, and scatter the plate with some of the caramelised walnuts.

018
ARTISAN RESTAURANT

22 The Weir, Hessle, East Yorkshire HU13 0RU

01482 644 906
www.artisanrestaurant.com

Artisan restaurant in Hessle, East Yorkshire, opened in 2004 and is solely operated and owned by husband and wife team, Lindsey and Richard Johns. Artisan is a unique and personal restaurant with space for sixteen guests. Richard cooks personally, without any other assistance, while Lindsey oversees the front of house. Artisan is a very welcoming and warm restaurant, which is reflected in the high levels of service and hospitality, Lindsey and Richard offer to their guests. Artisan is currently rated as one of the top dining destinations in Yorkshire. Artisan was recognised in the Top UK 100 restaurants 2008, a top 40 restaurant outside London and was Yorkshire restaurant of the year 2008/9. Artisan can also be found listed in most of the UK food guides, including the Good Food Guide. Richard takes advantage of the great Yorkshire larder, selecting the finest ingredients from very trusted suppliers. Richard then thoughtfully treats the produce in a style that allows the ingredients to shine through. Richard is a completely self taught chef, whereby the only two things that matter to him are high standards and satisfying his guests. Richard and Lindsey hope you enjoy the recipes.

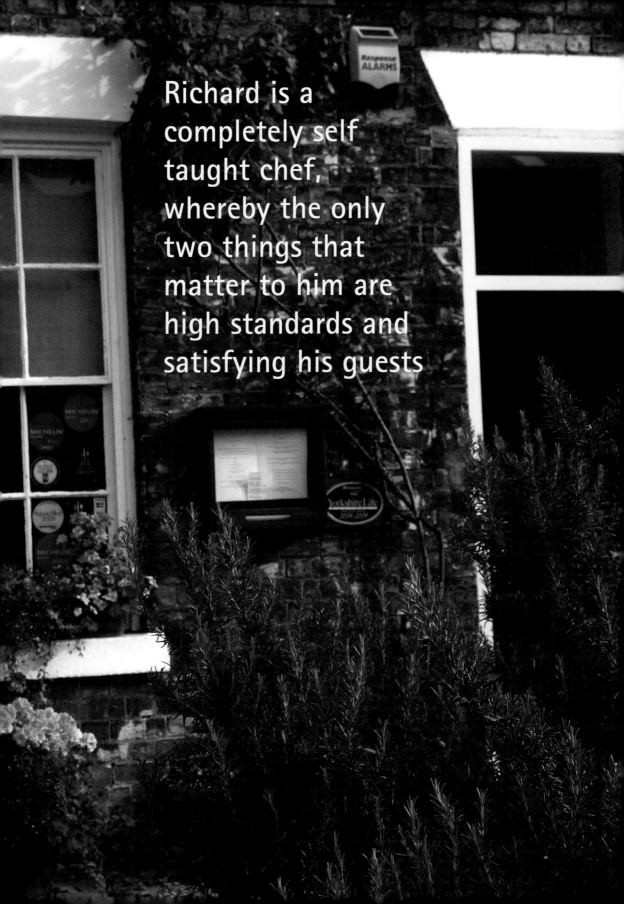

Richard is a completely self taught chef, whereby the only two things that matter to him are high standards and satisfying his guests

PAN SEARED SCOTTISH SEA SCALLOPS WITH APPLE PURÉE, APPLE CRISPS AND BACON

SERVES 4

Ingredients

12 very fresh king scallops, roe on
3 Granny Smith apples, 2 peeled, cored and chopped
Half used vanilla pod
100ml apple juice
Juice of 1 lemon plus zest
2oz butter
120g sugar
4 rashers of fine streaky bacon

Method

For the scallops

Clean scallops and take off roe (reserve roes to make fish sauce, soup, etc.)

For the apple purée

Place chopped apples, vanilla pod, 20g sugar, 1oz butter, apple and half lemon juice/zest in sauce pan. Cover and place on medium heat for approx 10 minutes or until apples are soft. Place apples in liquidizer until very smooth. Season to taste with salt and white pepper. Set aside.

Preheat oven 200°c. Place bacon onto tray and cover with baking parchment. Top with another tray. Place in oven for approx 10-15 minutes until crisp. Set aside.

For the apple crisps

These can be prepared well in advance. Add remaining sugar to 150ml water with half lemon juice. Bring to boil, simmer 5 minutes. Place apple slices in the mix to coat. Lay slices on non stick tray and leave in very low oven to dry out. Approx two hours. Place in airtight container.

Assembling the dish

Arrange apple purée on 4 warm plates. Heat frying pan until hot and add a little oil. Cook scallops until nicely coloured on each side. Remove and season with salt and pepper. Place scallops on apple purée and garnish each plate with crisp bacon and apple slices. Serve.

FILLET OF COD WITH WILD MUSHROOM, POTATOES, CAVIAR, BABY VEGETABLES AND A SHELLFISH SAUCE

SERVES 4

Ingredients

4 fillets of cod, or any white fish,
180g – 200g each
2 large potatoes, i.e Maris piper etc,
sliced into thick wedges
150g mixed wild mushrooms
Handful of chopped fresh herbs,
chives, parsley, tarragon
Selection of baby vegetables,
scrubbed and peeled
12 scallop roe, reserved from scallops
100g prawn shells or packet of ordinary prawns
1 onion, chopped
Clove garlic, crushed
300ml white wine
300ml fish stock
350ml cream
1tsp tomato purée
1 juice lemon
Olive oil to coat

Method

For the sauce

Cook onion in pan with a little oil until soft. Add garlic, tomato purée, roes and prawns. Cook gently for around 10 minutes. Add 300ml of wine and boil down until a syrup is formed. Add stock, boil down by two thirds. Add cream, bring to boil and simmer for 10 minutes. Season to taste with salt, pepper and a little lemon juice. Pass sauce through sieve. Set aside.

For the mushrooms and potatoes

Meanwhile, preheat oven 220°c. Fry mushrooms and set aside. Place potatoes in roasting tin and coat with olive oil. Roast in oven for 25 minutes until coloured and cooked. Add mushrooms to potatoes and mix well. Season. Set aside. Reheat in oven for a minute, before serving adding fresh herbs.

For the cod fillets

Season and place in a hot pan. Cook skin side down until coloured, finish in hot oven for 5 minutes, depending on thickness of fish. Finish with a squeeze of lemon juice. Whilst fish is cooking, place baby vegetables in salted boiling water and cook. Drain, toss in butter. Keep warm.

Assembling the dish

Divide potato mixture between 4 warmed plates, followed by vegetables. Spoon sauce over and around potatoes and vegetables. Top potatoes with cod and if using, a generous spoonful of caviar to finish. Serve.

VANILLA PANNA COTTA WITH FRESH BERRIES

SERVES 4

Ingredients

425ml double cream
290ml milk
1 fresh vanilla pod, cut in half and scraped
3oz caster sugar
2½ leaves sheet gelatine
1 punnet of fresh seasonal berries or fruit

Method

Soak gelatine in cold water for 5 minutes. Combine milk, cream, vanilla bean and sugar. Bring to boil, infuse for 20 minutes. Squeeze gelatine of water, add to cream. Stir into cream until dissolved. Pass mixture through a fine sieve and pour into suitable glasses or moulds. Keep vanilla bean for another use (apple purée recipe). Place in fridge for several hours, until set. Top with fruit of your choice. Serve.

028
THE BLUE BICYCLE

34 Fossgate York YO1 9TA

01904 673 990
www.thebluebicycle.com

Based in the centre of York, The Blue Bicycle is one of city's most talked about restaurants, where we serve award winning food in a relaxed dining atmosphere. We are highly commended for our fresh fish dishes, Homemade desserts and our extensive selection of fine wines.

At the turn of the century our cellar was a brothel of some repute. In fact if you wander downstairs, you will see photographs of some of the girls, who perhaps, plied their ware.

We now serve romantic dinners in the private vaulted booths (or beds), which are situated in the opulent and atmospheric dining area. You can enjoy a pre-dinner tipple overlooking the River Foss, reflecting on this bygone era of impropriety. The upstairs dining area exudes warmth and a busy atmosphere, with an eclectic range of tables and chairs, all beautifully presented. Lunch or Dinner with us is a high quality dining experience in exemplary surroundings, set in an intriguingly historic building, even by York's standards. We are totally committed to your comfort and relaxation and we pride ourselves on courteous attention to detail, a friendly approach and flexibility of service. We use the freshest ingredients, prepared and presented to the highest standards.

Situated along side the River Foss we also offer beautiful modern rooms. The Blue Rooms are luxurious, convenient, private and comfortable – perfect for leisure or business visitors or that short romantic break. The rooms have a cool minimalist feel with tasteful contemporary interiors.

Our wish is to ensure that the time spent with us is truly enjoyable and memorable, whether it is for a meal in our restaurant or a stay in the Blue Rooms. Please see our website www.thebluebicycle.com for further details.

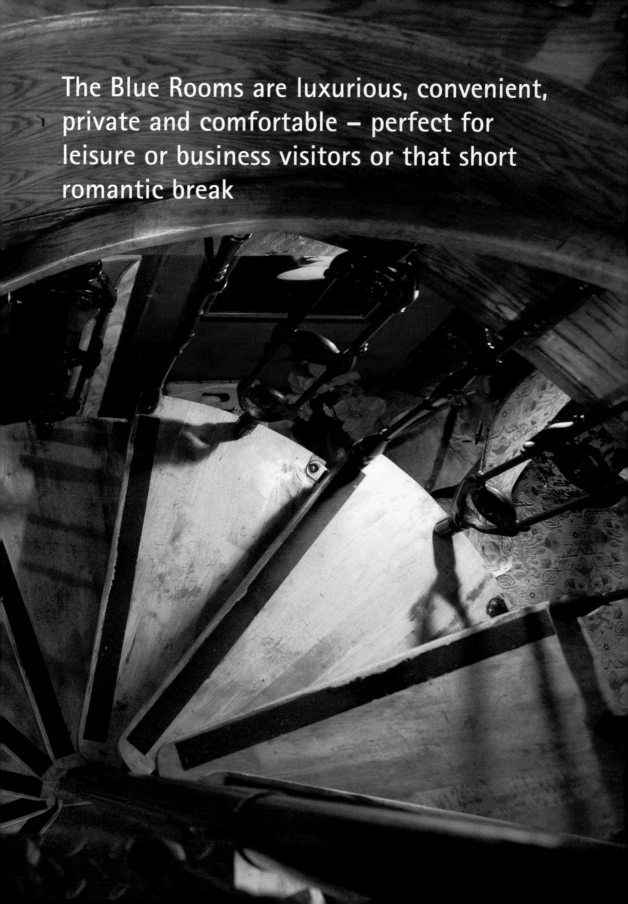

The Blue Rooms are luxurious, convenient, private and comfortable – perfect for leisure or business visitors or that short romantic break

SEARED SCALLOPS WITH GRUYERE AND CRAYFISH BONS-BONS, TOMATO, BASIL AND SAUCE VIERGE

SERVES 4

Ingredients

For the scallops
12 large king scallops
4tsp olive oil
Pinch of sea salt

For the bons-bons
250g crayfish
25g Gruyere, grated
Salt and pepper
2 egg yolks
50g breadcrumbs
25g flour

For the sauce vierge
100ml olive oil
1 lemon, juiced
3 tomatoes, concassed
2tbsp chopped basil
2tbsp chopped coriander
Salt and pepper

Method

For the bons-bons
Place the crayfish and the grated gruyere into a food processor and then season. Blitz until totally mixed. Then form into 12 small balls and refrigerate.

When cold coat them in the flour, then the egg yolk and breadcrumbs. Deep fry until golden brown.

For the sauce vierge
Gently warm the olive oil and lemon juice. Add the tomato, chopped herbs and season.

To serve
Pan sear the seasoned scallops in the oil for 45 seconds on each side in a hot pan. Place on a plate next to each bon-bon and drizzle the sauce over and around.

PAN-FRIED SEA BREAM WITH CONFIT FENNEL, POMMES DAUPHINOISE & A RED PEPPER, TOMATO & PERNOD COULIS

SERVES 6

Ingredients

For the sea bream
12 fillets sea bream
Sea salt and pepper
50ml oil

For Pernod coulis
100ml red wine vinegar
400ml tomato juice
100g caster sugar
3 red peppers
1 clove garlic, chopped

For the pommes dauphinoise
8 large potatoes
2pts cream
6 cloves garlic, finely chopped
Salt and pepper

For the confit fennel
3 large fennel bulbs
200ml vegetable oil
Sea salt and pepper

For the aromatics
3 cloves
2 bay leaves
2 sprigs of thyme
1 carrot, roughly chopped
1 onion, roughly chopped

Method

For the fennel
Slice the fennel bulbs in half and season with salt and pepper, cover with the oil and aromatics. Place in a low oven and cook for 1½ hours until tender.

For the Pernod coulis
This can be made sometime in advance. Apart from the caster sugar, blend all of the other ingredients together and pass through a muslin cloth into a thick bottomed pan. Then add the sugar and reduce on a low heat until you have reached a syrupy consistency.

For the pommes dauphinoise
Place the cream, garlic, salt and pepper in a thick bottomed pan and reduce by half. Peel the potatoes and slice as thinly as possible. Lay the sliced potatoes in a baking dish so that they cover the bottom of the dish. Then add a layer of the reduced cream. Repeat the process, making sure you finish with a neat layer of potatoes. Cover with foil and bake for one and a half hours at 180ºc. Remove from the oven and place a large weight on top of the potato and press until cool.

For the fish
Slice the fish into 6 portions. Then over a medium heat, warm a frying pan until it is very hot. To season the fish, make small cuts into the skin side of each of the sea bream fillets. This enables you to season both inside and outside of the fish and it will stop the fish curling up in the pan. Once seasoned drizzle the fish with oil and place the fillets skin side down into the pan. Cook for 6-8 minutes in total, first on one side and then turn the fish over.

To serve
Reheat the fennel and the potato and stack on the plate. Place the fish on top and drizzle the coulis around.

PEACH AND ALMOND WELLINGTON, WITH CLOTTED CREAM ICE CREAM AND HOMEMADE JAM

SERVES 4

Ingredients

For the wellington

2 ripe peaches

For the frangipane (almond filling)

50g butter
50g sugar
15g plain flour
50g ground almonds
1 egg
½ lemon, zest
½ orange, zest
1 vanilla pod
400g prepared puff pastry

For the jam

100g fresh raspberries
100g preserving sugar

For the ice cream

100g clotted cream
100g caster sugar
6 egg yolks
250ml milk
250ml cream
1tbsp liquid glucose
1tbsp glycerine

Method

Halve the peaches and roast for 10 mins at 180ºc, then allow to cool.

For the frangipane

Cream the butter and sugar, then add the egg and vanilla essence and whisk. Fold in the ground almonds, flour and lemon zest. Place in the fridge and allow to set. Once set place the frangipane into the peaches' stone cavities, roll out the puff pastry and wrap each individual peach in the puff pastry. Brush the pastry with some egg wash and dust with a little icing sugar. Place on baking tray and bake for 8-10 mins at 180ºc until golden brown.

For the jam

Place the fruit and sugar in a thick bottomed pan and cook at 120ºc until the sugar totally dissolves and thickens. Remove from the heat and leave to cool until it sets.

For the ice cream

Whisk together egg yolks and sugar until pale and fluffy. Warm the milk and cream until almost boiling, and then remove from the heat. Then add this mixture to the yolks stirring slowly, being careful not to split the eggs. Return the mixture to the hob on the lowest heat and warm until it thickens and coats the back of a spoon. Add liquid glucose, glycerine and clotted cream. Churn the mixture in an ice cream machine until soft set.

To serve

Place the wellington onto a plate, pour jam into glass jar and pipe ice cream on top. Decorate with fresh fruit and coulis.

038
THE BOX TREE

35-37 Church Street, Ilkley, West Yorkshire LS29 9DR

01943 608 484
www.theboxtree.co.uk

The Box Tree is one of the oldest buildings in Ilkley (circa 1720) and was first opened as a restaurant in 1963 by Malcolm Reid and Colin Long. The Box Tree quickly became the North's most successful restaurant. Simon and Rena Gueller took over the Box Tree in 2004 and have brought in a widely appreciated lighter touch to the place both in terms of décor and approach.

Over the last 5 years Simon and Rena Gueller, Andrew Pratt and their loyal team at the restaurant have been awarded numerous accolades including 3AA Rosettes, AA Notable wine list, Yorkshire Life restaurant of the year and the Michelin Star which has been retained for 5 years.

The modern French classical menu and extensive wine cellar offer food lovers an unforgettable experience. The Box Tree represents a combination of 21st century efficiency and exquisite good taste. Whilst the kitchens boast the latest equipment, the restaurant features a collection of art and antiques which define the style and luxury for which the Box Tree is famed.

Over the last 5 years Simon and Rena Gueller, Andrew Pratt and their loyal team at the restaurant have been awarded numerous accolades including 3AA Rosettes, AA Notable wine list, Yorkshire Life restaurant of the year and the Michelin Star which has been retained for 5 years

THE BOX TREE®

ROAST FOIE GRAS WITH PEACH MARMALADE AND GINGERBREAD CRISPS

SERVES 4

Method

For the peaches

Halve and stone the peaches, place in a pan with the basil leaves, lemon zest and a touch of water.

Put a securely fitting lid on top and cook very slowly in the oven at 140°c (check from time to time that it is not drying out in the pan, add more water if necessary).

When the peaches are cooked but still firm remove from the pan, peel off the skin. Roughly chop the peaches. Add vinegar to taste and season.

For the gingerbread

Thinly slice the gingerbread. Cut out with a ring into a disk. Brush with glucose syrup and bake at 110°c for 45 minutes. Carefully remove from the tray and curl round the handle of a wooden spoon.

For the marmalade

Warm up the marmalade in a pan and add 2 finely chopped basil leaves.

For the foie gras

Roast the foie gras in a pan on a medium temperature, season with Maldon salt.

To Assemble

Arrange the marmalade in a ring on the plate, place the foie gras and gingerbread crisps beside and garnish with small whole basil leaves, confit orange zest and a reduction of Cabernet Sauvignon vinegar.

Ingredients

4x 80g portions of foie gras
4 white peaches
6 basil leaves
1 lemon
10ml of Cabernet Sauvignon vinegar
Loaf of Jamaican gingerbread
Glucose syrup
Maldon salt
Confit orange zest
Thai basil leaves to garnish

ROAST LOIN OF VENISON, CELERIAC, FOREST MUSHROOMS, RED WINE SAUCE

SERVES 4

Ingredients

4x 150g portions of venison loin
1 celeriac
Selection of wild mushrooms
(morels, ceps, girolles)
½ bottle red wine
400ml veal stock
1 banana shallot
8 button mushrooms
Garlic
Thyme
Double cream
Butter
Savoy cabbage – cooked in butter
Deep fried thyme

Method

For the celeriac fondant

Cut out 4 nice thick squares of celeriac, cook in chicken stock and plenty of butter until tender, but still firm enough to hold its shape. To finish, (just before serving) sauté in butter to achieve a nice golden crust.

For the celeriac purée

With the remaining celeriac, dice into 2-3cm cubes and cook in half milk half water. When fully cooked through, strain and place celeriac in a new pan. Pour in double cream half way up the celeriac, reduce by half and blitz to a smooth purée (you may need to add a little more cream to get the correct consistency). Season with salt and white pepper. Add truffle oil and lemon juice to taste.

For the venison

Season and pan roast the loins, then place in a hot oven for 7-8 minutes, remove and rest for at least 7-8 minutes. Carve before serving.

For the sauce

Sauté 1 sliced shallot, 8 button mushrooms, 1 clove of garlic and thyme. Add half a bottle of red wine and reduce by half. Add 400ml veal stock, reduce by half again, pass through a sieve into a pan. Reduce this to sauce consistency when ready to serve and finish with 10g butter and a drop of double cream.

Assembling the dish

Drag the purée across the plate, place the golden fondant next to it, place some Savoy cabbage on the fondant and the carved venison on top of that. Arrange sautéed girolles, ceps and morels around the plate, and sauce, garnish with deep fried thyme.

CARAMELISED PINEAPPLE TART WITH SPICES,PHILADELPHIA SORBET, PINA COLADA

SERVES 4

Ingredients

200g sugar
100g butter
12 cloves
4 star anise
2 vanilla pods
2 pineapples
300 ml coconut milk
125 ml water
Gelatine leaf
Dark rum to taste
100g puff pastry
100g icing sugar
50g butter, soft
Cream cheese sorbet
Pineapple cigarette
Fresh mint

Method

For the pineapple and the pina colada

Skin the pineapple and cut into four discs, each an inch thick. Save the trimmings for the pina colada.

In a flat bottomed pan cook 200g of sugar with a drop of water until it caramelises and is golden brown. Add 100g of butter and mix. Stud each of the pineapple discs with 3 cloves and add to the pan.

Slice the vanilla lengthways and scrape the seeds out and add both to the pan along with the star anise.

Cook gently, turning frequently until the pineapple is tender and caramelised.

Blitz the pineapple trimmings until broken down, pass through a sieve and add rum to taste.

Take 300ml coconut milk and mix with 125ml water.

Soak one leaf of gelatine in cold water. Take a cupful of the coconut milk mix and gently warm in a pan. Squeeze out the gelatine and mix into the warm coconut milk. When the gelatine is fully dissolved add to the remaining mix of cold water and coconut milk. Whisk the mixture.

For the tart

Roll out the puff pastry in icing sugar until 3mm thick. Cut into 4 rectangles -15cm by 7cm. Prick with a fork and cover with icing sugar. Cook at 200ºc for approximately 15 minutes, until the pastry is cooked through and golden and glazed.

To assemble

Place the pastry disc on a plate over to one side leaving room for a shot glass, position the pineapple on top with the star anise and split vanilla pod on top, place cream cheese sorbet on to other side of the disc.

Fill a shot glass with the pineapple mix about two thirds up, top with the coconut milk (ideally with a cream whipper/ISI gun if you can get one). Place on the other side of the plate with a straw.

Drizzle the caramel from the pineapple around the plate ensuring you mix it around to get the vanilla seeds in it. Garnish with a mint tip and a pineapple cigarette.

048
THE BURLINGTON RESTAURANT

The Devonshire Arms Country House Hotel and Spa, Bolton Abbey,
Near Skipton, North Yorkshire BD23 6AJ

01756 718 111
www.thedevonshirearms.co.uk

The Burlington Restaurant at The Devonshire Arms Country House Hotel and Spa, Bolton Abbey is renowned for outstanding award winning food accompanied by one of the most remarkable wine lists in the country. A haven for complete relaxation and outstanding hospitality, the hotel is in a parkland setting on The Duke of Devonshire's 30,000 acre estate and surrounded by the glorious scenery of Wharfedale. The historic hotel has evolved over the centuries to provide today's guest with contemporary comforts in an atmosphere of grace and charm with supremely comfortable bedrooms and a choice of two restaurants - the celebrated Burlington, named after an ancestor of The Duke of Devonshire, and the vibrant Devonshire Brasserie and Bar.

At the helm of the Burlington is Steve Smith, a leading light of the northern cooking scene for more than fifteen years and over ten of those years with a Michelin star to his name. Calm, modest and thoroughly professional Steve produces ground-breaking food in a style that is both visually exciting and a thrill for the tastebuds.

Totally passionate about his craft, from good shopping for the best fresh seasonal produce to the final performance when guests are blown away by an exceptional imagination and artistry, the end result firmly benchmarks Steve as one of the country's top chefs. And whilst chefs' reputations may be built on stars and awards, of which Steve has notched up his fair share, he says, "What really matters is that my diners enjoy a fantastic meal and want to return again and again." And they do.

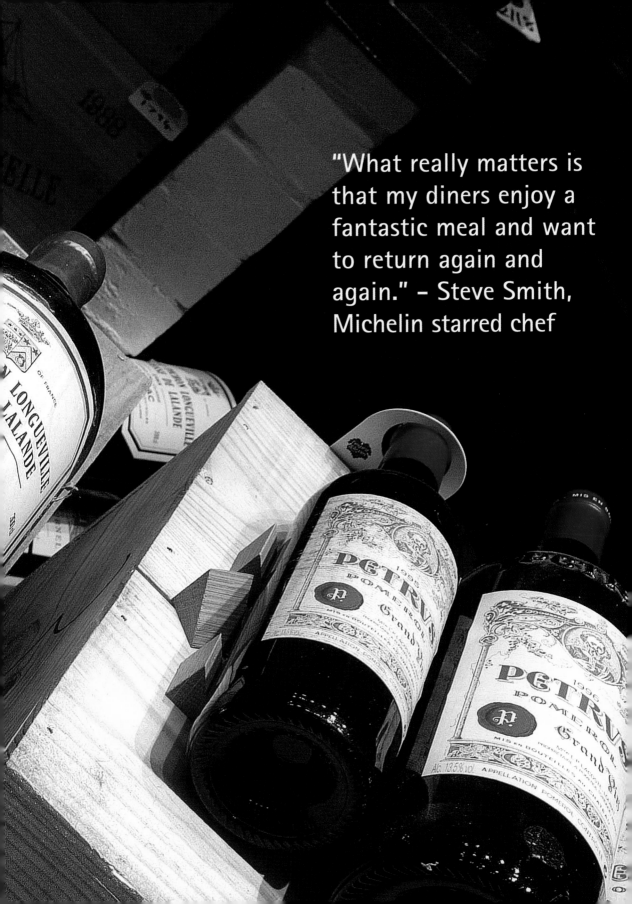

"What really matters is that my diners enjoy a fantastic meal and want to return again and again." – Steve Smith, Michelin starred chef

GOOSNARGH DUCK TEXTURES, DUCK LIVER PARFAIT, FIG FLUID GEL

SERVES 4

Ingredients

Goosnargh duck confit roll

4 Goosnargh duck legs
1 shallot, chopped
2 tbspn parsley, chopped
1 tspn capers, chopped
1 tspn gherkins, chopped
100ml duck stock
Salt and pepper

Smoked duck breast

1 Goosnargh duck breast
Salt and pepper

Air dried duck breast

1 Goosnargh duck breast
500g sea salt
50g sugar
1 strip orange
2 juniper berries

Gizzards

100g duck gizzards
200g salt
400g duck fat
1 garlic clove
1 sprig thyme
1 sprig rosemary

Duck liver parfait

300g duck livers
3 eggs at room temperature
100ml port
25ml Madeira
25ml brandy
200g butter, melted at room temperature
50g shallots, sliced
1 sprig thyme

Fig fluid gel

300ml fig juice
30g isomalt
3g gallen gum

Method

For the Goosnargh duck confit roll

Remove the duck meat from the legs, place into a mixing bowl. Add all other ingredients and mix to combine. Season to taste.

Spread some cling film onto a work top and place the duck mix along one side of it. Roll to form a cylinder. Tie the ends and place in the fridge to set.

For the smoked duck breast

Slowly cook the duck breast in a non stick pan, skin side down to render the fat. Once the fat is crisp and golden brown, place into a smoker and smoke for 8 minutes. Remove and allow to cool. Slice into thin slices and reserve until needed.

For the air dried duck breast

Blend the salt, sugar, orange and juniper berries together. Cover the duck breast with the mix and leave in the fridge. Marinate for 8 hours. Remove the breast from the salt and wash off. Dry the breast and hang in a cool place for 5 to 7 days. When the breast has dried slice thinly.

For the gizzards

Cover the gizzards with salt and marinate for 4 hours. Wash the salt off and dry. Place in an earthenware pot, cover with the fat. Add the herbs and garlic. Cook for 8 hours on 90°c. Remove and allow to cool. Store and use as required.

For the duck liver parfait

Place the shallots, herbs and alcohol in a pan and reduce to a syrup. Allow to cool. Place the reduction, duck liver and eggs into a blender and blend till smooth. Gradually pour in the butter. Season to taste.

Place into an earthenware pot and cook in a bain-marie for 1 hour at 95°c. Remove and allow to cool. Place in the fridge to set. Serve as required.

For the fig fluid gel

Place all ingredients in pan and heat to 90°c. Cool the liquid to 37°c. Place in a blender and blend together. Store and use as required.

To serve

Serve as the picture, garnish with a few pea shoots.

LAMB WITH BROCCOLI AND TOMATO

SERVES 4

Ingredients

Lamb
1 double best end of lamb
4 large vac pack bags
75g butter
Salt

Stock
Lamb trimmings, from the double beat end
Lamb fat, rendered from the best end
75ml white wine
Water to cover
1 sprig of rosemary
2 clove of garlic
1 celery stick
½ onion
1 tomato
50ml vegetable oil

Sauce
Lamb stock
Remaining lamb trimmings
50ml of Noilly Prat
1 tomato, chopped
½ lemon
½ sprig rosemary
½ garlic clove
10g butter
Salt

Method

For the lamb

Bone down each side of the back bone to expose the lamb loin. Bone down to the rib bones. With a cleaver, chop through the ribs to leave 2 lamb loins on the bone. Remove the skin and expose the lamb fat. Score with a sharp knife. Trim the lamb into French trim with the bone exposed by 2½cm at the top. Remove the first and last bone to leave a 6 bone lamb rack. Keep all trimmings to make the stock and sauce. Render the lamb fat trimmings to obtain a clear lamb fat. Cool. When cool divide between 2 vac pack bags. Place some tin foil over the exposed lamb bones at the top of the lamb racks. (This is to stop the bones from potentially piercing the vac pack bag). Lightly season the lamb best end and place into the vac pack bag. Vac at the highest mb pressure possible. Place the lamb into a water bath set at 65°c for 40 minutes 1 hour before serving. Remove from the water bath and allow to rest for 5 minutes. Remove from the vac pack bag and pat dry. Season the lamb. Render the fat side of the lamb in a cold pan and allow the heat to increase to colour and render the fat. Cook the fat until it is golden brown and crisp. When cooked put the lamb in a cold pan and cook the skin until crispy. Remove from the pan and allow to rest. Carve between the lamb bones to produce 6 cutlets, serve as required.

For the stock

Chop all the trimmings into small pieces. Roast in a hot tray with some of the rendered lamb fat, roast until golden brown. Place into a colander and drain any excess fat. Deglaze the pan with white wine. Use a wooden spoon to remove as much of the caramelised meat juices as possible. Pour through a small tea strainer and reserve. In a pan sweat the mirepoix until golden, again drain in a colander to remove excess fat or oil. Add ingredients together, use two thirds of the lamb trimmings, in a pan, bring to the boil. Skim constantly to remove impurities from the stock. Simmer for 30 minutes. Pass the stock through a chinois and then through double muslin twice. Reduce by half.

For the sauce

Place the stock, Noilly Prat, tomato and remaining lamb trimmings into a pan and bring to the boil. Skim if required. Add the rosemary and garlic, reduce by half. Pass sauce through muslin and return to a pan. Adjust seasoning with salt and lemon juice if required. Just before serving melt a little butter into the sauce.

To serve

Re heat the purée and spoon to one side of the plate. Arrange 5 pieces of gnocchi per portion on the plate. Slice the lamb and arrange next to the purée. Pour the sauce into a sauce boat to be served at the table.

APPLE PIE PARFAIT, BLACKBERRY JELLY, APPLE SORBET

SERVES 4

Ingredients

Apple pie mousse

400ml double cream
4 egg yolks
80g caster sugar
90g apple purée
3 gelatine leaves
400ml double cream, semi-whipped

Blackberry jelly

1ltr blackberry purée
400ml water
14g agar agar

Granny Smith apple jelly

250ml apple purée
250ml apple juice
5g agar agar

Apple sorbet

1ltr apple boiron purée
1ltr apple juice
600g caster sugar
200g trimoline
10 drops Granny Smith flavouring
3 drops lime green food colouring

Method

For the apple pie mousse

Whisk eggs and sugar, bring cream to the boil, pour over eggs, cook out, add gelatine and purée, allow to cool but not set, fold in cream, allow to set, pipe into cylinders and tie.

For the blackberry jelly

Whisk ingredients into a pan, allow to stand for 10 minutes, bring to a boil, set onto trays weighing at 333g per tray.

For the Granny Smith apple jelly

Warm apple purée and apple juice, pass, allow to cool, add agar agar, bring to the boil, add flavouring and colouring, set in bread loaf tin, cut into 1cm.

For the apple sorbet

Bring apple juice, sugar and trimoline to a boil, pour over boiron, whisk, pass, allow to completely cool, add drops, churn.

058 CLOCKTOWER

Rudding Park, Follifoot, Harrogate, North Yorkshire HG3 1JH

01423 871 350
www.ruddingpark.co.uk

f food is your passion, then look no further than Clocktower; with modern British menus using local, seasonal ingredients, served in stunning surroundings. Dine in the restaurant underneath the striking pink glass chandelier, relax in the bright and airy conservatory alongside the 400 year old olive tree or simply enjoy a drink at the cosmopolitan bar.

Clocktower offers a fun and lively, yet relaxed experience for everyone, no matter the occasion. Clocktower is one of the most popular restaurants in North Yorkshire, recognised not only for its excellent menu but also for its enjoyable atmosphere and passionate, friendly staff.

After your meal, coffee can be taken in the comfortable surroundings of the Mackaness Room where guests can unwind with a drink and the daily newspapers, or a range of board games.

As well as the Clocktower restaurant, Rudding Park offers 50 executive bedrooms, extensive conference and banqueting facilities, an 18 hole parkland Hawtree course and a 6 hole Repton Short Course with a replica of the notorious 17th at Sawgrass, Florida.

If food is your passion,
then look no further
than Clocktower, serving
modern British menus
using local, seasonal
ingredients

WHITBY CRAB, CRAYFISH AND AVOCADO COCKTAIL WITH LACEYS TRADITIONAL CHEESE WAFER

SERVES 4

Ingredients

To create this dish you will need 4 Martini glasses

2 dressed Whitby crabs, white crab meat only
1 ripe avocado
20 cooked crayfish, shelled
2 baby gem salad leaves
150g finely grated Lacey's traditional cheese

Dressing

100g caster sugar
Finely grated zest of 2 limes, using a micro plane if possible
Juice of 2 limes, passed through a sieve
Water to mix

Method

For the dressing

Using a very clean pan (if your pan is not very clean the sugar will crystallise) place the sugar in the pan and just cover with water. Heat this until a thick syrup like consistency is reached, and then add the lime juice and zest to the syrup. Allow this thick lime dressing to cool.

For the wafer

Simply place the grated cheese on baking parchment or a silicone mat and bake gently at 160°c for 5 minutes until golden and crisp. Remove from the tray and allow to cool.

Chefs note: This will not work with all cheeses but if you want an alternative Parmesan cheese works really well.

Assembling the dish

Wash, dry and polish your Martini glasses and place on a tray.

Rinse and pat dry the little gem salad leaves with a clean cloth then shred with a knife and place into the bottom of the Martini glasses. Pick through the cooked dressed Whitby crab (discarding any shell) and place on top of the little gem salad in each glass.

Place 5 crayfish on top of the crab-meat, then spoon over the lime syrup dressing.

Serve with the Lacey's Traditional wafer on the side of the glass.

RACK OF NIDDERDALE LAMB WITH MINTED PEA PURÉE, LOCAL BABY CARROTS, SERANO HAM GRATIN, PEA SHOOTS AND RED WINE JUS

SERVES 4

Ingredients

4x 4 bone racks of lamb, French trimmed, ask your butcher to do this for you
150g fresh or frozen peas
4 stems of mint, leaves removed and washed, then pat dry with a clean cloth
12 local baby carrots, peeled with tops removed – pre-cook the carrots in salted water and refresh under a cold tap when cooked
4 baking potatoes, peeled
300ml double cream
2 cloves of garlic, peeled and finely chopped
6 slices of Serano ham, chopped
150g Gruyere cheese, crumbled
2pts strong lamb stock
1 large glass of red wine
100 g butter
2 punnets of pea shoots
3 shallots, peeled and finely chopped

Method

For the gratin

Put the crushed garlic and double cream in a pan and bring to the boil. Remove from the heat and allow to cool.

Next, peel the potatoes and cut into thin slices. Then layer the potatoes in an earthenware dish with slices of Serano ham in between. As you build up the dish, spoon over the garlic cream mixture between each of the layers, gently season. Remember that Serano ham is quite salty.

Finally top with the grated Gruyere cheese. Bake in a hot oven at 180°c for 30-40 minutes until the potatoes are soft.

For the lamb

Season the racks of lamb with salt and pepper, seal in a hot pan and then place in the oven for 15 minutes until cooked. Take out and allow to rest before slicing.

For the peas

Cook the peas until soft, add the mint, then using a small hand held stick blender purée them until soft.

For the carrots

Cook in boiling water for approximately 2 minutes, strain, then toss in butter.

For the jus

Put the chopped shallots into a pan with a tablespoon of oil and fry for approximately 5 minutes, then add the wine to this and leave to simmer until reduced by half.

Add the stock and continue to reduce until a thick sticky dark sauce has formed. This should give you enough sauce for the 4 plates.

Assembling the dish

Cut the Serano ham gratin potatoes into small round towers with a cutter and place on the 4 hot plates.

Carve the racks of lamb into 2 and intertwine the bones of the lamb so they stand upright like a guard of honour!

Spoon the purée onto the plate, add the carrots then finish the plate off with a sprinkle of pea shoots.

PUDSEY RHUBARB TASTER

SERVES 4

Ingredients

Rhubarb crumble

4 sticks of rhubarb
1 cup of water for cooking
Small earthenware dish, enough for
4 small portions
1 vanilla pod, split and seeds removed
100g caster sugar

Crumble

200g flour
110g unsalted butter
110g caster sugar
Finely grated zest of 1 lemon
5 plain digestive biscuits, crushed
1tbsp of flaked almonds

Rhubarb lassi

2 sticks of rhubarb
100g caster sugar
2 pots of natural full fat yoghurt

Rhubarb cheesecake

100g ginger nut biscuits
40g unsalted butter, melted
90g cream cheese
60g sugar for the cream mix and 20g for
the rhubarb
90g sour cream
90g whipped cream
4g gelatine
70g rhubarb

Rhubarb syrup

100ml water
200g sugar
100g rhubarb, chopped

Jelly glaze

500ml water
500ml sugar
1 stick of rhubarb, chopped
8 leaves of gelatine

Method

For the rhubarb crumble

Chop the rhubarb and place in a pan with the sugar, water and vanilla then cook at 180°c until the mix is soft and has begun to stew slightly. Keep this to one side while you make the crumble.

In a separate dish, mix the flour and butter together. Add the caster sugar (saving some to sprinkle on the top at the end) Next, add all the other ingredients and stir well. Gently put the crumble on top of the rhubarb, and sprinkle some sugar on top. Bake at 180°c for half an hour or until cooked.

For the rhubarb lassi

Place the rhubarb in a pan with some water and the caster sugar, keep on a medium heat until the rhubarb has softened. Drain, but keep the juice and the pulp and allow both to cool separately. Place the two emptied contents of the yoghurt pots into a bowl, add the rhubarb pulp and slowly add the juice. Then gently blend with a stick blender to form a refreshing drink. Serve in shot glasses.

For the rhubarb cheesecake

Break the biscuits into crumbs by placing them in a bag and beating with a rolling pin. Add the melted butter and mix and then press into the base of 4 individual round moulds. Chop the rhubarb into chunks and place in a pan with 2 tablespoons water and 20g sugar. Place on the heat for 6-8 minutes until very soft. Leave to cool. Beat the cheese, sugar and sour cream until smooth. Add the stewed rhubarb followed by the melted gelatine. When the mix is cool fold in the whipped cream and set in the prepared moulds on top of the biscuit base. Place the cheesecake in a tray to set and cut out with a clean knife into diamond shape for the plate for service.

To make the syrup, boil the water and sugar, then add the chopped rhubarb. Simmer for 5 minutes, remove from the heat and pass through a fine sieve. The syrup may need to be reduced further depending on its consistency; it should be a thick mixture.

For the jelly glaze

Heat the water and sugar in a pan, add the rhubarb and cook for approximately 15 minutes. Remove the rhubarb and discard. In a separate dish, soak the gelatine leaves in cold water for approximately 3 minutes, then, once soft add to the still warm rhubarb syrup, stir until dissolved. Allow to cool slightly before pouring a thin layer on top of the cheesecake then chill until set.

To assemble (this pudding looks great on a long thin plate)

Place the shot glass at one end and secure with a small blob of whipped cream to stop the glass rolling around. Then place the diamond of cheesecake in the centre. Then place the rhubarb crumble at the other end. Pour a swirl of syrup around the cheesecake and serve.

068
THE FOURTH FLOOR
AT HARVEY NICHOLS

107-111 Briggate, Leeds LS1 6AZ

0113 204 8000
www.harveynichols.com

The Fourth Floor at Harvey Nichols Leeds, offers a luxury bar and both à la carte and prix fixe menus plus a wine list featuring over 200 wines and champagne from around the world. The Fourth Floor Café & Bar is open every day, and stays open for dinner five nights a week, when the rest of the store is closed.

A wall of floor-to-ceiling windows that look out over the rooftops of the city, and open onto a balcony area defines the stunning interior.

By day The Fourth Floor is spacious and airy, flooded with sunlight. By night it transforms into a more intimate space altogether, with lower lighting and twinkling small candles adorning every available surface.

The food reflects the elevated position seasonal menus use the best Yorkshire and the region have to offer with dishes from breakfast through to dinner and afternoon tea in-between.

The bar area, with its club-style leather seating hits the right note for comfort and style, and our skilled bar team can design the coolest of bespoke cocktails with which to greet guests on arrival.

Used to dealing with customers at the highest levels, the staff at The Fourth Floor provide service that not only pays attention to every minute detail, but which is fun and dynamic at the same time.

By day The Fourth Floor is spacious and airy, flooded with sunlight. By night it transforms into a more intimate space altogether, with lower lighting and twinkling small candles adorning every available surface

SLOW COOKED PORK BELLY, SEARED SQUID, MUSHROOMS AND ORANGE

SERVES 4

Ingredients

250g Yorkshire outdoor pork belly
200ml chicken stock
20ml soy sauce
2 fresh medium squid, cleaned but
with tentacles
100g smijie mushrooms, a small
Japanese mushroom
1 small pak choi
50ml orange juice
40ml olive oil
1 star anise
1 cinnamon stick
Pinch of sesame seeds

Method

For the pork belly

This is best done in advance. You can keep it refrigerated once cooked, until you need it. Ask your butcher to score the skin of the pork belly. Season the belly well with salt and pepper, then in a hot pan sear gently on the skin, then flip over on to the meat side. Place in a roasting dish skin side up and pour over the soy and the chicken stock so that the liquid just covers the pork. Cook at 130ºc for around 1½ hours until tender and soft. Now place a flat board or pan on top of the pork to press lightly and chill in the stock. Cut the pork belly into around 5cm squares once cold.

For the squid

Now cut the squid remove the tentacles then save and cut the body in half, long ways. Cut the body into strips about two fingers thick.

Put the orange juice the star anise and the cinnamon in a pan and boil rapidly until thick. Cut the pak choi into quarters and trim the mushrooms slightly.

To cook

Warm a flat pan until hot and carefully place the belly pork pieces skin side down in it, cook quickly then place in a hot oven. In a new pan cook the squid pieces quickly for 1-2 minutes moving them the whole time. Add the mushrooms and pak choi to the pan.

To serve

Place the hot crisp pork belly on the plates then arrange the squid in-between. Scatter the mushrooms around and then the pak choi. Finally, drizzle the orange juice reduction and the sesame seeds.

RELISH YORKSHIRE
THE FOURTH FLOOR AT HARVEY NICHOLS

DALES LAMB WITH HOTPOT SHOULDER BEETROOT SAUCE GRILLED LEEKS

SERVES 4

Ingredients

6 bone rack of lamb, ask for French trimmed

300g lamb shoulder fat removed

100g plain flour

1 onion

2 potatoes

8 baby leeks

2 cooked beetroot

2ltrs good lamb stock

Method

For the hotpot

First to make the hotpot you will need 4 shallow dishes no bigger than 8cm and around 5cm deep. Cut the lamb into finger nail size pieces these can be various shapes. Cut the onion into half, and then into slices, in a shallow heavy pan slowly cook the onion until golden brown with a little butter adding a little lamb stock if it becomes dry. Now add plenty of white pepper to the flour and a little salt. Now dust the lamb pieces lightly in the flour shaking off excess in a sieve.

In a roasting tray heat a tablespoon of vegetable oil until hot now fry the lamb pieces quickly in the oil until each is golden brown. Drain the lamb well and then return to the tray after wiping the tray with some kitchen roll. Pop in the lamb and add enough stock to just cover stir well and place in the oven at 130°c for around 30 minutes, reserve the rest of the stock. When cooked mix with the onions and set aside. Peel the potatoes and keep in cold water.

Place the lamb and onion mix in your small pots. Slice the potatoes thinly and layer on top of lamb mix brush with butter and place in oven.

For the rack of lamb

Season well with salt and pepper then sear the outside until golden brown. Place with the skin side up on a roasting tray and roast at 180°c for 15 minutes. Meanwhile dice the cooked beetroot in to small dice. Warm up a chargrill pan or your grill, lightly oil the baby leeks and grill lightly on both sides.

For the beetroot sauce

Now remove the rack from the oven and rest in a warm place for a few minutes out of the tray. Pop the beetroot in the roasting tray from the rack and add a splash of the lamb stock. Boil until reduced and thick. Check the hotpots, the potatoes should be golden brown and the lamb piping hot. Now carve the lamb down the bone and place on plates with a hotpot and grilled leeks. Add a little beetroot sauce.

PLATE OF AMPLEFORTH APPLE DESSERTS

SERVES 4

Ingredients

The apples we use for this dessert come from the monks at Ampleforth Abbey where they also make the wonderful apple brandy!

This is a plate of miniature apple desserts here is a selection of those shown.

Apple panna cotta

200ml double cream
200ml milk
45g sugar
2 leaves gelatine
40g fresh apple purée

Apple crumble

2 apples
1tsp Yorkshire honey
1tbsp caster sugar
1 cinnamon stick
100g Demerara sugar
200g plain flour
80g porridge oats
160g unsalted butter, diced

Caramelised apple frangipane

2 small apples
50g caster sugar
1 small vanilla pod, seeds scraped out
1tsp honey

Frangipane

(This amount will make a little more than you need but it freezes well)
225g soft butter
225g caster sugar
225g ground almond
25g plain flour
4 whole eggs

Method

For the apple panna cotta

You will need some small presentation dishes for this, about 5cm deep and 4cm wide.

Bring milk, cream and sugar to a gentle boil. Soak the gelatine in cold water for five minutes add the now drained gelatine to the milk and cream mix, whisk and gently add the apple purée.

Strain the mixture through a fine sieve cool the mixture over a bowl of ice when thick pour into your dishes and set in the fridge for 2 hours .

For the apple crumble

Peel and core the apples, dice, pop in a roasting tray with a small splash of water and add the caster sugar, cinnamon and honey and cook in the oven at 160ºc until apple is soft but not puréed. Cool slightly.

For caramelised apple frangipane

Peel and core apples, slice thickly then place in a roasting dish. Pour over rest of ingredients and place in an oven on 150ºc. Until golden and soft.

For the frangipane

Cream the butter and sugar together in a mixer until light and fluffy. Beat the eggs together in a bowl then add a little at a time to the butter mixture beating after each drop. Add the flour and ground almonds and mix well to combine. Chill this mixture well

Take 4 small pudding basins or mini muffin trays. Grease well, and spoon the frangipane mixture in place and add half a caramelised apple slice on top. Bake in oven at 160ºc until golden for around 15 minutes. Take out of mould once cool.

To assemble

Place one of each dessert on a oval plate with a further slice of the caramelised apple.

078
THE GENERAL TARLETON INN

Boroughbridge Road, Ferrensby, Knaresborough HG5 0PZ

01423 340 284
www.generaltarleton.co.uk

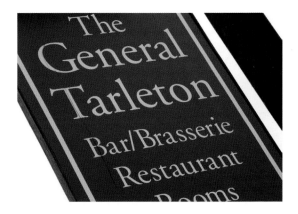

Built in the 18th Century, The General Tarleton at Ferrensby started life as a traditional coaching inn. John Topham, who grew up just 6 miles away, was keen to return to the area and spotted the potential of the General Tarleton. After 18 years at the celebrated, Angel Inn in Hetton, his decision to go it alone has resulted in what is now, an award winning inn with rooms.

The General Tarleton's 'Food with Yorkshire Roots' menu changes with the seasons and celebrates the abundance of superb local produce on the doorstep. One thing the GT is never short of is choice – Lamb from the Yorkshire Dales, Birstwith Beef, Nidderdale Salmon, Whitby Crab and game from the Ripley Estate just up the road. The commitment to local Yorkshire ingredients is clear for all to see and 75% of produce comes from within 30 miles of the Inn.

Fish is a firm favourite at the GT and one of John's signature dishes are Little Moneybags, a selection of seafood in a crisp pastry bag with lobster sauce - people travel miles for them.

There's always a warm welcome at The General Tarleton and it's certainly worth staying overnight especially when you are greeted with a pot of tea, homemade Yorkshire Curd Tart and in the bedroom, some of Aunt Bertha's homemade biscuits.

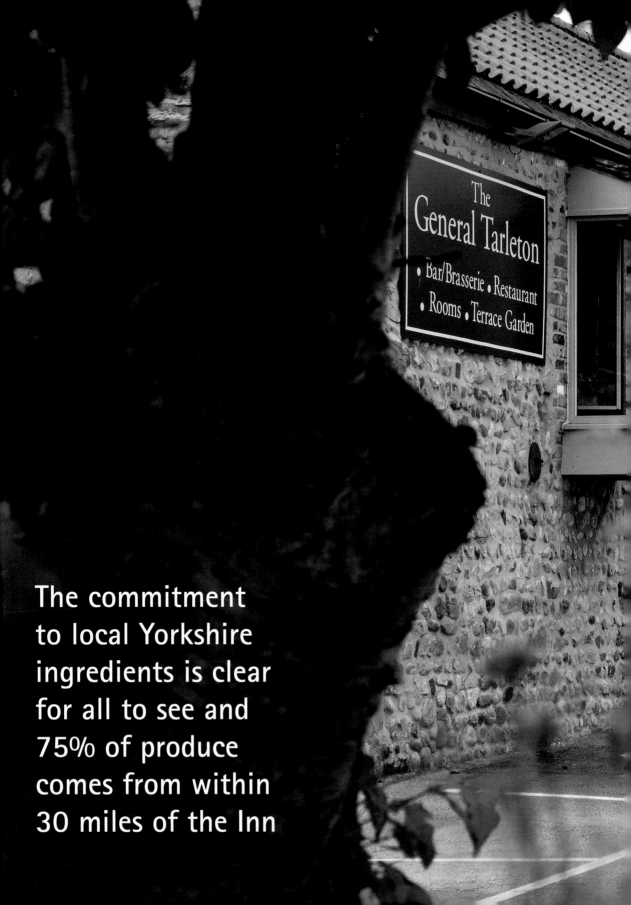

The commitment
to local Yorkshire
ingredients is clear
for all to see and
75% of produce
comes from within
30 miles of the Inn

GRILLED BLACK PUDDING WITH POACHED FARMHOUSE EGG, CRISP BACON AND BLACK SHEEP ALE DRESSING

SERVES 4

Ingredients

8 slices black pudding
4 very fresh farm eggs
4 slices dry cured streaky bacon
100g spinach
½pt Black Sheep ale
100g sugar
Dash lemon juice

Method

For the dressing

Place the ale and sugar in a saucepan and reduce to a syrup, finish with lemon juice and leave to cool.

For the bacon

Heat the oven to 180°c, sandwich the bacon between parchment paper and two flat trays, bake until crisp.

For the eggs and black pudding

In a large pan of water, add a dash of vinegar and salt, bring to a rolling boil and poach the eggs. While poaching the eggs, grill the black pudding and sweat the spinach.

Assembling the dish

To serve, divide the spinach between 4 plates, sit a poached egg on top, add the black pudding and bacon then drizzle with the Black Sheep dressing.

ROAST PARTRIDGE WITH ANISE PEAR AND YORKSHIRE BLUE CHEESE RAREBIT

SERVES 4

Method

For the pears
Gently poach the pears in a syrup of the sugar, lemon juice, star anise and water and cook until tender.

For the croutons
Cut the bread into a crouton shape and gently fry until crisp and golden, reserve in warm place.

For the partridge
Rub the partridge with butter, season and insert thyme sprigs in the cavity.

In a hot pan, colour the birds on all sides then roast in a hot oven for 10 minutes.

Remove the birds from the roasting tray and rest, keeping warm.

For the blue cheese
Deglaze the roasting pan with port then chicken stock and reduce to sauce consistency. Meanwhile, place the blue cheese onto the croutons and glaze under a hot grill.

Assembling the dish
Place partridge on a warm plate along with the rarebit crouton, poached pear and sauce.

Ingredients

4 oven ready partridge
30ml port
400ml chicken stock
30g butter
Sprigs of thyme
4 slices white bread
100g Yorkshire blue cheese, or similar
4 pears
4 star anise
Juice of 1 lemon
200g sugar

CINNAMON BRULEE, HEDGEROW BLACKBERRY AND APPLE CRUMBLE, PLUM AND VANILLA COMPOTE

SERVES 4

Ingredients

Brulee

4 egg yolks
570ml double cream
110g sugar
1tsp ground cinnamon
Sugar to glaze

Plum compote

8 plums, halved and stoned
200g sugar
1 vanilla pod, seeded
1 orange zest and juice
1 star anise
Lolly sticks cut in half

Crumble

2 bramley apples
20 blackberries
200g crumble mix

Method

For the brulee

Bring cream to boil. Cream the sugar, cinnamon and egg yolks and pour over the hot cream, whisk and return to the pan over a low heat stir with a wooden spoon until you have a nice, thick custard. Pour into brulee moulds and set in the fridge. Glaze before serving.

For the compote

Place all ingredients into a pan, gently bring to the boil and cook until soft. Check sweetness and leave to cool.

For the crumble

Skin and dice apple, add sugar and cook in a pan until soft. Add the blackberries and divide between small individual pots and top with crumble mix. Bake in moderate oven for 8 minutes.

To Assemble

To assemble dish, glaze the brulee while cooking the crumble, add compote to a shot glass and top with ice cream. Place all 3 individual puddings on a plate and serve.

088
HOTEL DU VIN AND BISTRO

Prospect Place, Harrogate HG1 1LB

01423 856 800
www.hotelduvin.com/harrogate

Located close to the centre of the historic North Yorkshire spa town of Harrogate. The Hotel and Bistro overlooks the Stray, a 200-acre common, created in 1778 by an act of Parliament and containing many of Harrogate's famous mineral springs.

Occupying a row of eight Georgian styled houses, the Hotel is home to the trademark Bistro Restaurant; a relaxing haven serving stunning culinary classics.

Murray Wilson head chef at the Bistro recently attained 2 rosette awards after only 11 months and at the tender age of 25.

Murray a former Masterchef the professionals' finalist prides himself on using local producers and suppliers; sourcing as much as he can from within a 30 mile radius of Harrogate.

The Bistro boasts an extensive wine list of over 550 bins; you are guaranteed to have the perfect wine to match your meal courtesy of our dedicated in house sommelier team.

We can also cater for many different requirements; menus can be created upon request for wedding parties and private dining. We also have an exciting and very popular wine dinner calendar throughout the year.

The Bistro boasts an extensive wine list of over 550 bins; you are guaranteed to have the perfect wine to match your meal courtesy of our dedicated in house sommelier team

DIVER CAUGHT SCALLOPS, ARTICHOKE PURÉE, PANCETTA

SERVES 4

Ingredients

12 hand dived scallops, cleaned and
roe removed
300g Jerusalem artichokes
200ml cream
100ml milk
100g butter
4 thin slices pancetta
Salt to taste

Method

For the artichokes

Working quickly peel the artichokes and slice thinly, place in a pan and cover with the milk and cream, cook on a medium heat until soft. Add the butter to the pan and blend until smooth, season to taste.

For the pancetta

Place the pancetta on an oven tray lined with greaseproof paper. Pre set oven to 100ºc place in the oven for around 30 minutes, or until they are crispy.

For the scallops

Heat a non stick pan with a touch of oil until hot, just below smoking point. Cook the scallops for 1½ minutes on one side, turn over and add the butter. Cook for a further minute and half, they should be golden brown.

Season and serve.

ROASTED YORKSHIRE RABBIT
CARROTS, CREAMED SAVOY, POTATOES

SERVES 4

Ingredients

4 large rabbit saddles, with kidneys
8 slices Parma ham
8 Chantenay carrots
2 large carrots, peeled and thinly sliced
350ml cream
75ml milk
150g butter
12 ratte potatoes
1 head of savoy cabbage, outer leaves removed
and inner leaves very thinly sliced
Salt to taste

Method

For the rabbit

Lay 2 slices of Parma ham on cling film, place the rabbit saddle on top and put kidneys in the middle of the saddle. Roll very tightly in the cling film and leave in fridge.

For the ratte potatoes

Cook the ratte potatoes in salted water until they are just cooked, chill and slice each potato into three.

For the carrots

Cook the sliced carrots in 150ml of the cream and all the milk until soft, blend until smooth with 50g of the butter, season to taste. Place the Chantenay carrots in water and boil until soft.

For the cabbage

Use the remaining cream and 50g butter place in a pan and reduce by half, add the sliced savoy cabbage and cook until soft.

To cook the rabbit and potatoes

Pre heat oven to 200ºc add some vegetable oil to a roasting tray and heat in the oven. Remove the rabbit saddles from the cling film and once the tray is hot place the saddles in to seal the outer sides, then add the sliced cooled ratte potatoes.

Finally

Leave in the pre heated oven for 5 minutes turning occasionally. Remove from the oven and add the remaining butter to the tray, baste the rabbit and potatoes for a minute or so.

COCONUT PANNA COTTA, CHARGRILLED PINEAPPLE

SERVES 4

Ingredients

Panna cotta
300g coconut purée
1 sheet gelatine, soaked in water
50g white chocolate
1tbsp Malibu

Chargrilled pineapple
1 pineapple, cut into 5cm x 5cm squares
1 vanilla stick, seeded
300g sugar
150ml white wine
150ml water

Method

For the panna cotta

Gently heat the coconut purée until very hot, then whisk in the soaked gelatine. Place the white chocolate in a mixing bowl and pour the coconut gelatine mix over. Blend well then add the Malibu. Pass the liquid through a fine sieve and set in moulds overnight.

For the pineapple

Combine 150ml sugar, water and white wine in a pan and bring to the boil, simmer for 5 minutes then remove from the heat. Place the remaining sugar in a heavy based frying pan with the vanilla, heat until light brown caramel in formed, add the pineapple and cook for 2 minutes on one side then turn and repeat. Add the wine syrup and poach gently until the pineapple is soft, chill. When ready to serve chargrill the pineapple and serve with the panna cotta.

To serve

Add shaved coconut and some mango sorbet to serve.

098
THE MAGPIE CAFÉ

14 Pier Road, Whitby, North Yorkshire YO21 3PU

01947 602 058
www.magpiecafe.co.uk

Situated on the harbour side in the beautiful ancient fishing port of Whitby The Magpie Café is ideally placed to make the most of the abundance of fresh fish and seafood the North Sea has to offer. At least a dozen varieties of fresh fish are on offer most days including Prime Cod, Lemon Sole, Halibut, Wild Sea Bass, Turbot to name a few plus Local Crab and Lobster, Lindisfarne Oysters and of course the Famous Whitby Kipper.

The restaurant offers a very informal family friendly setting to relax and enjoy the food from a menu that whilst predominantly piscine, offers something for everyone. There is also an excellent wine list and some twenty homemade desserts.

Whitby born Head Chef Paul Gildroy and his team have a wealth of experience and are constantly thinking of new ways to serve the locally sourced produce from Gods own county of Yorkshire.

Although the restaurant can seat in excess of one hundred and twenty people it is set out over a series of rooms so never feels too big and has a homely ambience.

The restaurant offers a very informal family friendly setting to relax and enjoy the food from a menu that whilst predominantly piscine, offers something for everyone

WHITBY CRAB PATE WITH AUBERGINE CHUTNEY
SERVES 4

Ingredients

For the pate

375g brown crab meat
175g white crab meat
1 medium onion, roughly chopped
1 clove of garlic, crushed
50ml merlot
100g crème fraiche
125g chilled butter
1tsp parsley, chopped
2tbsp oil
Black pepper

For the aubergine chutney

1kg aubergines, chopped into 1 centimetre dice
500g bramley apples, roughly chopped
1 large onion, finely diced
400g dark brown soft sugar
200ml white wine vinegar
2tsp ground ginger
1tsp coriander seeds
½tps mixed spice
1tsp salt

Method

For the chutney

Place all the ingredients into a pan over a low heat and let the sugar dissolve, bring to the boil and then turn down to a gentle simmer, cook for between 1-1½ hours, stirring occasionally, or until thick and has a sticky gelatiness feel to it.

Once it has cooked place into sterilised jars cool down and store in the fridge.

For the pate

Heat the oil in a shallow frying pan and add the onion and garlic, gently sauté until soft and translucent. Add the brown crab meat, merlot and crème fraiche and cook over a medium heat until liquid is reduced by a third (approx 10-15 minutes).

Remove from the heat and pour into a food processor and blitz until smooth, slowly add the chilled butter blitz to mix well.

Pass the blitzed crab through a sieve into a bowl and fold in the white crab meat and chopped parsley, taste and adjust the seasoning as required.

Chill for a minimum of 4 hours or preferably overnight.

MAGPIE SEAFOOD PAN HAGGERTY

SERVES 4

Ingredients

1½kg peeled potatoes, use Estima or another
waxy variety which should not break up
1 large onion, finely sliced
200g black pudding
1ltr chicken stock
350g fresh mussels
250g fresh clams
150g queen scallop meat
250g wild sea bass fillet, pin boned
and cut into 4
250g haddock fillet, pin boned and cut into 4
250g gurnard fillet, pin boned and cut into 4
8 medium sized crevettes
2tbsp parsley, chopped
Salt and pepper
Oil for cooking

Method

First slice the potatoes (no more than half a centimetre thick), in a frying pan heat a little oil and sauté the sliced onion, colouring a little.

Layer the onion into a large deep frying pan or baking tray with the potatoes, lightly seasoning each layer, pour over the stock, cover with foil and place into a preheated oven (200ºc) for about 30-40 minutes or until the potatoes are tender. Remove from the oven and crumble in the black pudding and add the mussels, clams, crevettes and the queen scallops (push the mussels and clams into the potato to get the flavour into the gravy).

Cover with foil and return to the oven for a further 10 minutes or until the mussels and clams open and the crevettes are pinkie orange in colour. Remove from the oven and taste for seasoning, set to one side covered with the foil. Heat a little oil in a frying pan, season the fish and carefully lay in the pieces of fish flesh side down starting at the top of the pan going clockwise around.

After about 1 minute turn each piece of fish over and cook for a further minute.

To serve

Remove the foil from the potatoes and place the pan fried pieces of fish on top of the potatoes, sprinkle with the chopped parsley and serve immediately with wedges of lemon.

RICH CHOCOLATE MOUSSE WITH CINDER TOFFEE PIECES

SERVES 4

Ingredients

For the mousse

275g good milk chocolate pieces
100g good dark chocolate pieces
300ml full cream milk
3 leaves of gelatine
600ml double cream

For the cinder toffee

250g granulated sugar
4tbsp golden syrup
50ml water
1tbsp malt vinegar
2tsp bicarbonate of soda
Oil for greasing

Method

For the mousse

Warm the milk in a saucepan to just below boiling point, remove from the heat and pour in both lots of chocolate, stir until melted and mixed thoroughly. Place the leaves of gelatine into cold water and leave for a minute or two until softened, drain and squeeze out any excess water from the gelatine and add to the milky chocolate, stir until dissolved. Transfer to a bowl and leave to cool. Once this has cooled it should have started to thicken up slightly (do not allow to set), whip up the double cream to a soft peak (any further and you risk the cream splitting whilst folding into the chocolate). Very gently fold the whipped cream into the chocolate, place into a fridge to set.

For the cinder toffee

First line a baking tray with baking parchment and very lightly oil the parchment. In a large heavy based pan place the sugar, water, vinegar and golden syrup, gently heat until the sugar has dissolved, then turn up the heat and boil until the syrup turns a deep caramel colour (the darker you let the syrup go, the more of a bitter taste it will have) you could use a sugar boiling thermometer and boil to the caramel stage, remove the pan from the heat and whisk in the bicarbonate of soda, this should make the toffee erupt, hence the reason for using a large pan, pour immediately into a greased lined baking tray, allow to set, then break with a rolling pin. Store in an airtight container until ready to use.

To save time a good alternative is to use Mr Cadbury's Crunchie bars

To serve

Place the set mousse into a piping bag and pipe a little mousse into the bottom of a glass coupe and sprinkle with the cinder toffee, repeat this so you have layers of mousse and toffee, finish off the dessert with a little whipped cream and more sprinkles of cinder toffee, serve immediately.

RELISH YORKSHIRE
THE MAGPIE CAFÉ

MIDDLETHORPE HALL & SPA

National Trust

Bishopthorpe Road, York YO23 2GB

01904 641 241
www.middlethorpe.com

Middlethorpe Hall is a William and Mary country house, built in 1699. It was bought in the 1980s and reopened as a luxury hotel, restaurant and Spa in 1984. The restoration, conservation and conversion into a Country House Hotel has been carried out to exacting and historically accurate standards.

The house has been elegantly decorated in the manner of the 18th Century and furnished with antiques and fine paintings, so that its look and ambiance is that of a well-kept, well-furnished private manor house rather than a 29 bedroom hotel. In September 2008, Middlethorpe Hall and Spa became the inalienable property of the National Trust by donation, with all profits benefiting the houses and the charity.

Guests can relax in the panelled dining rooms overlooking twenty acres of manicured gardens and enjoy antiques reflecting the tastes of several centuries. The dining room is an oasis of calm, where guests leisurely dine overlooking the magnificent view of the gardens and parkland. Nicholas Evans' superb cuisine at Middlethorpe Hall as well as its extensive wine list have won many accolades over the years, and continue to attract connoisseurs of fine food and wine from around the world. As well as the award winning restaurant, private dining rooms, which are ideal for wedding parties, business entertaining or family celebrations. There is also a Health and Beauty Spa which contains a large indoor swimming pool, spa bath, steam room, sauna, gymnasium. Three beauty salons with qualified therapists complete the offering.

Guests can relax in the panelled dining rooms overlooking twenty acres of manicured gardens and enjoy antiques reflecting the tastes of several centuries

POACHED TURBOT FILLET, ROAST SCALLOPS, BABY LEEK, GIROLLES, ROAST CAULIFLOWER PURÉE, FINE BEANS AND ROAST CHICKEN SAUCE

SERVES 4

Ingredients

4 70g turbot fillets
4 diver caught scallops
4 baby leeks
24 small girolles
24 fine beans
1 small cauliflower
100ml roast chicken sauce
250g butter
250ml light chicken stock
Olive oil
Sea salt
Pepper
Lemon juice

Method

For the cauliflower purée

Cut the cauliflower into small florets and place in a roasting tray, lightly coat in olive oil and season with salt and pepper and roast in a 160°c oven until the cauliflower is tender and the cauliflower has started to brown. Remove from the oven and place in a food processor. Purée the cauliflower until smooth, add diced butter to loosen the cauliflower, season and pass the purée.

For the turbot

Butter a baking dish and place the turbot in the dish, season and cover with chicken stock. Place tin foil over the tray and bake in a 160°c oven, bake until the fish is firm to the touch. Remove the scallops from the shell and then remove the skirts, wash and dry the scallop and then pan fry in olive oil until golden brown, when cooked season with lemon juice and salt and pepper.

For the baby leeks, fine beans and girolles

Blanch the baby leeks, fine beans in boiling salted water until the vegetables are tender. Remove from the water and glaze with butter.

Gently pan fry the girolles in olive oil and butter until the girolles are cooked, season with lemon juice and salt and pepper.

Warm the chicken sauce and blitz with a hand blender to emulsify.

To serve

Plate as per picture and garnish with dark green sakura cress.

**RELISH YORKSHIRE
MIDDLETHORPE HALL & SPA**

ROAST LOIN OF VENISON, FONDANT POTATO, CEPS, SHALLOTS, BOK CHOI, MUSHROOM PURÉE, TRUFFLE SAUCE

SERVES 4

Ingredients

4 140g venison loin, trimmed
4 potato cylinders
4 fresh ceps
250g button mushrooms
50g shallots, finely sliced
30g dried ceps
30g double cream
12 shallots
15g sugar
1 tbsp sherry vinegar
2 bok choi
30g black truffle
150ml venison sauce
250g butter
4 garlic cloves
6 thyme sprigs
Sea salt
Pepper

Method

For the potatoes

Finely slice butter and place in the base of a saucepan. Place the potatoes flat side down on top of the butter, season with salt and pepper, garlic and thyme sprigs. Gently heat the pan until the butter starts to foam, when the potato is golden brown on the base remove from the heat and leave to cool for 5 minutes. Turn the potatoes and gently heat again until the base of the potato is golden brown and cooked.

For the mushroom purée

Melt 100g of butter in a large pan and add the sliced shallots and gently cook until the shallots are tender, add the sliced mushrooms and dried ceps and cook until the mushrooms are golden brown and tender. Add the double cream and bring to the boil. Place the mushrooms into a food processor and purée until smooth, season and then pass.

For the shallots

Peel the shallots and then place in a pan with 50g of butter, thyme sprigs, sugar, salt and pepper. Add enough water to cover the shallots half way. Place on the heat and bring to the boil and cook until the water evaporates. When the water has evaporated deglaze with a tablespoon of sherry vinegar.

For the ceps

Trim and clean the ceps and then slice. Pan fry the ceps in olive oil and a little butter. Season with salt and pepper and lemon juice

Trim the bok choi and then blanch in boiling salted water until the bok choi is tender.

For the venison

Season the venison and then pan fry in olive oil and butter, cook until the venison is golden brown all over and to your own liking. Leave the venison to rest and then slice and season and serve

Warm the venison sauce and add chopped truffle to the sauce.

Plate as per picture and garnish with finely sliced truffle.

PEAR CHARLOTTE, CARAMEL MOUSSE AND VANILLA ICE CREAM

SERVES 4

Ingredients

4 comice pears
8 slices white bread
250g butter
150g caster sugar
200g sugar
1 cinnamon stick
30g cinnamon powder

Ice cream

500g whipping cream
500g milk
200g egg yolks
40g glucose
80g trimoline
200g sugar
2 vanilla pods

Caramel sauce

1½ cinnamon sticks
½ heaped tsp cumin seeds
100g unrefined caster sugar
40g unsalted butter
100g double cream

Caramel mousse

1 tin condensed milk, boil for
4 hours and then cool
500ml double cream
1 leaf gelatine

Method

For the pear charlotte

Place 100g of butter and 30g of cinnamon powder into a food mixer and whip until light and fluffy. Butter the bread and then remove the crusts, cut into strips and line a non stick mould with the butter on the outside against the mould.

Peel and slice the pears and then make a caramel sauce with sugar, butter, water and the cinnamon stick. Add the pears and cook until the pears are tender then chill. When the pears are chilled place into the moulds and top with another slice of buttered bread, cover the tops of the moulds and then bake at 170°c for 15 minutes or until the bread is crisp and golden.

For the ice cream

Whisk the egg yolks and sugar until white and fluffy, bring the milk, cream, trimoline, glucose and vanilla to the boil and then pour onto the egg yolks, return to the pan and cook out until the custard coats the back of a spoon, pass and chill for 24 hours. Whisk the custard and then pour into an ice cream machine and then churn until thick and creamy. The ice cream is then stored in the freezer until needed.

For the caramel sauce

Dry roast the cinnamon stick and the cumin seeds on the stove, over a gentle heat for 5 minutes, add the cream and then level to infuse. In a second pan gently warm the sugar until it becomes a golden caramel add the diced butter and stir in. Add the cream and spice mix and simmer for 3 minutes and then pass and store until needed.

For the caramel mousse

Place a tin of condensed milk in a pan of cold water and then bring the water to the boil and then simmer for 4 hours, topping up with water if needed. Leave in the pan to go completely cold. When cold open the tin and place in a bowl, whisk the condensed milk caramel until smooth, dissolve a sheet of soaked gelatine in a little cream and then add to the caramel, add the cream and then whisk until firm, store in the fridge until needed.

To serve

Reheat the pear charlotte in the oven and the plate as per picture.

118
OLIVE TREE
GREEK RESTAURANT

188-190 Harrogate Road, Chapel Allerton LS7 4NZ |
55 Rodley Lane, Rodley LS13 1NG | **74-76 Otley Road, Headingly LS6 4BA**
01132 698 488 | 01132 569 283 | 01132 748 282
www.olivetreegreekrestaurant.co.uk

Established in 1982, The Olive Tree group of family owned restaurants has grown over the years and there are now three in West Leeds. The restaurants are run day to day by the husband and wife team George and Vasoulla, while George busies himself in the kitchen overseeing his talented team of chefs; Vasoulla takes care of the front-of-house team and helps them maintain their exceedingly high standards.

The couple are Greek Cypriot born but consider themselves very much to be adopted Yorkshire folk, they moved to West Yorkshire over 35 years ago and raised their two children here, Vicki and Solos. Solos is now involved with the business and is quickly learning all the skills necessary to run and develop a group of quality minded restaurants.

George is a self-taught chef and recognises his mother-in-law as one of his most important influences. He holds her philosophy of 'real ingredients cooked by real people' very close to his heart and believes we should go back to the way our grandmothers cooked, using only the best ingredients each season has to offer and cooked in an honest wholesome manner.

George has developed his talent over many years cooking for his many regular customers, friends and of course family, a bit like a really good Kleftiko - which happens to be one of George's specialities.

The dynamic combination of talents has propelled the restaurants into the media spotlight and helped them receive many excellent reviews and awards right from the start. Most recently the readers of

Let's Eat Leeds magazine voted The Olive Tree as 'The Best Mediterranean Restaurant 2005/6'.

Once again after many years The Olive Tree was featured in the latest Which? Good Food Guide, the AA restaurant guide, Relais Routiers and has received high acclaim from the Egon Ronay Guide.

The press have taken great interest with AA Gill of The Sunday Times pronouncing that The Olive Tree was in the top four Greek restaurants in the country, great reviews have also come from Robert Cockroft of The Yorkshire Post, plus the Telegraph, the Argus and Yorkshire Life. George has also appeared on television promoting and teaching about Greek food including BBC 2's 'Food and Drink' show three times, ITV's 'This Morning', Yorkshire Television, Cyprus Television and most recently cooking on Sky. Whenever George and Vasoulla are promoting or cooking Greek food they are always striving for the best results from the best ingredients. Good publicity seems to stick to them like great Baklava (another of George's specialties!), we hope you see why!

"The Olive Tree is in my top four Greek restaurants in the country" – AA Gill

GARIDES SAGANAKI (BAKED PRAWNS WITH TOMATOES AND FETA)

SERVES 4

Ingredients

In Greece, where this dish is called yiouvetsi the prawns are cooked in their shells as this keeps them moist and juicy and the dish is served warm rather than hot. You may peel the prawns if you like before you cook them, leaving the tails on. Saganaki is a round earthenware baking dish in which the prawns are cooked and this is what the dish takes its name from.

4 tablespoons olive oil
1 onion, finely chopped
4 garlic cloves, crushed
1 bunch spring onions with the green parts, finely chopped
½ red and ½ yellow peppers, seeded and cubed
750g ripe tomatoes, peeled seeded and roughly chopped
A pinch of sugar
1 tablespoon fresh oregano leaves or
½ teaspoon dried oregano
or 1 tablespoon fresh thyme leaves or
1 teaspoon dried thyme
Juice of ½ lemon
60ml dry white wine
450g raw tiger prawns, thawed if frozen and peel with the tails intact
A small bunch of fresh flat leaf parsley, finely chopped
125g feta cheese, cubed
Sea salt and freshly ground black pepper

Method

For the sauce

Preheat the oven to 180ºc, gas mark 4. Over a medium heat, heat the oil in a large heavy frying pan and when hot but not smoking fry the onion gently for 2-3 minutes until translucent. Add the garlic, spring onions and pepper and cook, stirring occasionally for 2-3 minutes longer.

Stir in the tomatoes, sugar, oregano or thyme, lemon juice and wine and season to taste. Cook gently over a low heat for about 10-12 minutes stirring occasionally until the sauce reduces slightly and thickens.

For the prawns

Stir the prawns and parsley into the tomato sauce. Divide the prawns and sauce into individual oven proof dishes. Sprinkle the feta cubes on top.

To cook

Bake in the preheated oven for 8-10 minutes until the prawns are pink and the feta has just melted and is lightly browned. Sprinkle with parsley and serve hot with plenty of crusty bread to mop up the juices.

KLEFTIKO (BAKED LAMB WITH OREGANO)

SERVES 4

Ingredients

This is a traditional Greek classic
made with lamb shanks or meat pieces
from the shoulder of lamb with the bone
left in. Kleftiko is slow-cooked with
herbs until it literally falls off the
bone developing a meltingly tender
texture and fragrant flavours.

60ml extra virgin olive oil
Juice of 1 lemon
4 pieces of lamb, approximately 500g each from
the shoulder or leg of lamb, with the bone left
in, trimmed of all fat
4 cloves garlic, cut into thin slivers
2tsp cinnamon
2tsp dried oregano
A small handful of fresh oregano
coarsely chopped
4 bay leaves
125ml red wine
Salt and freshly ground black pepper

Method

For the lamb

Preheat the oven to 220°c/Gas 7.

Mix the olive oil and lemon juice in a small saucepan and brush
all over the lamb pieces.

With a sharp knife make 4-5 small slits on both sides on every
piece of kleftiko and insert slivers of garlic into every slit.

Sprinkle ½ a teaspoon of cinnamon and ½ teaspoon of
oregano and a quarter of the chopped fresh oregano on both
sides of the lamb pieces. Season well and place a bay leaf on
top of each piece.

Wrap the kleftiko pieces loosely in foil and fold to make a parcel.

Place in a small tray, fill with hot water a third of the way up.
Pour the wine in and place the tray in the oven.

Bake for ½ an hour, turn the kleftiko pieces over, turn the oven
down to 160°c /Gas 3 and bake for a further 1½ hours or
until the lamb is golden brown and tender and almost falls off
the bone.

To serve

Serve with roast or boiled potatoes and a Greek salad.

BAKLAVA

MAKES 24 PIECES

Ingredients

This is a popular sweet, nut filled pastry. Although the origins of this dessert are from Greece and Turkey it can be found in the Balkans, Northern Africa and the Middle East.

250g walnuts , coarsely chopped
250g blanched almonds, coarsely chopped
75g pistachio nuts, coarsely chopped
Finely grated rind of 1 lemon
2 teaspoons cinnamon
4-5 cloves, ground
75g unsalted butter
125ml vegetable oil

For the syrup

600ml water
350g caster sugar
75g clear honey
2 strips of thinly pared lemon rind
1 stick cinnamon
4-5 whole cloves

Method

Preheat the oven to 180°c/Gas 4. Mix the nuts and lemon rind with the cinnamon and cloves in a small bowl. Melt the butter with the oil in a small pan and using a pastry brush lightly grease the base of a shallow 30 x 20 cm baking tin. Line the baking tin with 1 sheet of pastry, folding over any excess pastry. Brush this lightly with the melted butter and oil. Repeat until you have used half of the pastry sheets, brushing each one lightly with butter and oil.

Spread half the nut filling over the pastry and cover with 3 layers of the filo pastry, brushing the butter and oil on each layer. Sprinkle the remaining filling over the pastry.

Add the last sheets of filo pastry on top again brushing butter and oil over each sheet. Fold any excess pastry underneath to keep the top tidy and finally brush the top of the pastry liberally with butter/oil, making sure that you cover the whole surface.

Dip a sharp knife into boiling water and score through the first four sheets making squares or diamond shaped portions. Sprinkle the top sheet of pastry with water to prevent it curling upwards.

Bake in the preheated oven for 1 hour or until golden brown.

Take the baklava out of the oven and let it cool before adding the syrup.

Meanwhile, make the syrup, place the water in a small saucepan with the sugar, honey, lemon rind, cinnamon and cloves. Bring to the boil and simmer uncovered for 15 minutes until the mixture has thickened slightly. Take the syrup off the heat and let it cool slightly.

Discard the lemon rind and spices and pour the hot syrup over the cooked pastry. Leave to soak for a few hours or overnight before cutting into portions. Serve decorated with chopped pistachio nuts.

Baklava keeps well in the refrigerator for up to 1 week.

128
SAMUEL'S AT SWINTON PARK

Swinton Park, Masham, Ripon, North Yorks HG4 4JH

01765 680 900
www.swintonpark.com

For something truly inspiring, the dining room at Swinton Park with its ornate gold leaf ceiling and sweeping views really will take your breath away. This wing of the castellated castle was built in 1890 by the current owner's great-great-great grandfather, and helps create a truly memorable dining experience. The food itself, though, is also cause for celebration.

Guided by the experienced hand of Head Chef, Simon Crannage, the freshness and quality of the ingredients speak for themselves, the style of cuisine being Modern British with a strong seasonal bias. The commitment to "gate to plate" and low food miles is taken seriously here, and most of the ingredients will have been sourced from the hotel's own four acre walled garden, or from the surrounding 20,000 acre estate (also in the ownership of the Cunliffe-Lister family).

The castle is the stately home of the Earl of Swinton and oozes tradition and grandeur, whilst at the same time offering every contemporary comfort you would expect of a first class hotel. Service is discreet and attentive, and the lavishly furnished drawing room and sitting room, with blazing fires in winter and a terrace and croquet lawn in the summer, entice every guest to linger over an afternoon tea or after dinner coffee. Each of the 30 bedrooms is individually designed, with an exclusive use spa and five treatment rooms for those in need of a little pampering. There is also a wide range of country pursuits on offer, including falconry, golf and fishing.

For those wanting to extend their culinary skills, the cookery school runs evening, day and residential courses throughout the year, and the Chef's Table demonstration dinners at weekends are particularly popular.

Recent accolades include Taste of Yorkshire (White Rose Awards 2007), AA 3 Rosettes and Hotel of the Year (White Rose Awards 2009)."

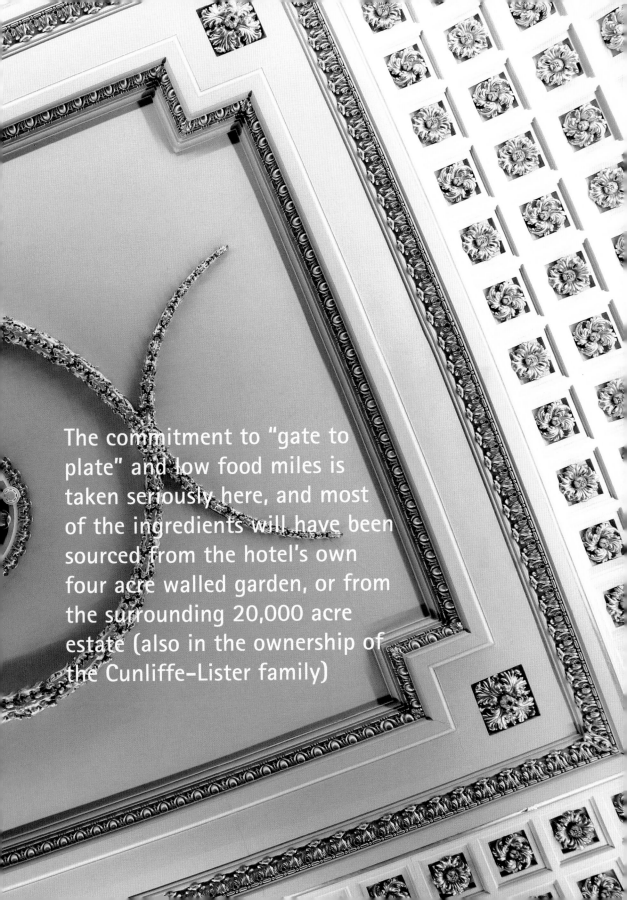

The commitment to "gate to plate" and low food miles is taken seriously here, and most of the ingredients will have been sourced from the hotel's own four acre walled garden, or from the surrounding 20,000 acre estate (also in the ownership of the Cunliffe-Lister family)

FILLET OF NORTH COAST BLACK BREAM, ARTICHOKE GRATIN, WATERCRESS CREAM

SERVES 6

Ingredients

3 whole black bream, scaled and filleted

Artichoke gratin

8 large Maris Piper potatoes, peeled and
thinly sliced
1kg Jerusalem artichokes, peeled and
thinly sliced
500ml milk
500ml double cream
2 cloves of garlic, crushed
1 sprig rosemary
Salt and pepper

Method

For the artichoke gratin

Put the milk, cream, garlic and thyme into a large pan, season well with salt and pepper, bring to the boil then remove from the heat and allow to infuse for 20 minutes. Line a baking tray with greaseproof paper. First place a layer of sliced potato on the bottom of the tray then place a ladle of the cream mix onto the potatoes, repeat the process again using the artichoke. Continue to alternate the layers until the baking tray is full or about 10cms high. Place the filled tray into a preheated oven 180°c and cook for 90 minutes. Allow to cool. For the best result you can place another tray on top of the gratin and press lightly. Once chilled, cut into desired shape and reheat in the oven at 180°c for 6 minutes.

To cook the fish

Ask your fishmonger to fillet the bream and remove all the bone for you. Cut each fillet into three pieces. Heat a non stick frying pan with a little oil in it, season the fish with salt and pepper then place the fish skin side down into the hot pan, cook for 3 minutes until the skin is nice and crisp, turn the fish over then remove from the heat. The residual heat in the pan will finish the cooking, squeeze a few drops of lemon to finish and serve.

Serving suggestions

In the restaurant we serve with this dish, some vegetable ribbons dressed in a little lemon juice and truffle oil. Also we serve creamed watercress as a sauce which gives the dish a vibrant colour.

SWINTON ESTATE VENISON, BRAISED HAUNCH FORESTIERE, BEETROOT FONDANT, WALLED GARDEN SQUASH PURÉE

SERVES 6

Ingredients

Haunch forestiere

1kg Braised venison haunch, finely shredded, braised in beef stock until tender
250g mixed wild mushrooms
100g pancetta lardons
2 shallots, finely diced
1 clove of puréed garlic
Sliced Parma ham for wrapping

Beetroot fondants

4 Large beetroot, cut into discs
500ml water
100ml red wine vinegar
1 clove of garlic, crushed
1 sprig of thyme
50g sugar
Salt and pepper

Method

For the haunch forestiere

Reduce the cooking stock down until very thick and add this back to the meat, venison haunch can be very dry so this adds a little moisture to the meat. In a large pan warm some vegetable oil and add the pancetta, shallots, garlic and mushrooms. Sweat for 4 minutes and add to the meat mix. At this point check the mix for season and adjust to your own preference. Roll into cylinders using cling film and set in the fridge. Once the mix is firm remove the cling film and wrap the cylinders in Parma ham. Re-wrap in cling film again. To reheat, cut the cylinders into required size and put into a hot oven for 12 minutes, you can leave the cling film on to hold its shape. It won't melt in the oven.

For the beetroot fondants

Add all the ingredients into a pan, bring to the boil and simmer for 1 hour until the beetroot is tender, you can do this in advance and reheat in the liquid when needed.

Serving suggestions

In the restaurant we also serve a silky garden squash purée, sautéed kale and a piece of the venison loin with this dish.

DARK CHOCOLATE MARQUISE WITH GARDEN BRAMBLES

SERVES 6

Method

For the chocolate marquise

Melt the chocolate, butter and cocoa powder over a pan of hot water in a glass bowl. Put the egg yolks, sugar and cream in a bowl and whisk until light and fluffy, then fold the melted chocolate mix into the egg yolk mix and fill desired moulds and chill in the fridge until set.

For the blackberry jelly

Soak the gelatine in cold water until soft. Place all ingredients into a large pan and warm until all ingredients have dissolved together; pour into a shallow tray lined with cling film and chill until set. Cut into desired shape.

Serving suggestions

In the restaurant we serve rosemary ice cream. Fresh brambles and a sprig of mint to garnish.

Ingredients

Chocolate marquise

400g dark chocolate
800g butter
250g cocoa powder
360g egg yolks
400g sugar
400g cream

Blackberry jelly

350g blackberry coulis
150g cranberry juice
250g nappage, hot
32g gelatine leaves

138
THE WESTWOOD RESTAURANT

New Walk, Beverley, East Yorkshire HU17 7AE

01482 881 999
www.thewestwood.co.uk

Situated in the historic market town of Beverley, between York and Hull in the heart of the East Riding of Yorkshire, the Westwood Restaurant stands proudly as an exciting modern, destination restaurant for neighbourhood foodies.
A short walk from the Westwood Pasture, which offers stunning views of Black Mill, the Race Course and Beverley Minster, The Westwood is easily accessible by road or rail.
Located in the grounds of Beverley's old courthouse, a Grade II listed Georgian building, and shielded from the road by a 200 year old Acer tree, The Westwood provides an elegant setting for all occasions. With a courtyard sun terrace – perfect for summer alfresco dining - and an ample private car park, The Westwood is one of the jewels in the region's restaurant scene.

On the first floor, with the stunning backdrop of an oak encased wine wall, there is a private dining area that seats up to twenty four. Guests can choose bespoke set menus, for that special occasion, with a little help from the experienced kitchen team. Downstairs there is a chef's table for 6 guests overlooking the kitchen team at work, a great spot for enthusiasts to watch the experts and pick up some insider secrets.
Showcasing simple yet stylish food, Matthew, Michele and their team aim to use high quality, locally sourced ingredients to evolve their seasonal menus.

Cooking for Matthew is about getting the best out of the ingredients on offer, delivering beautiful plates packed with great flavour.
Renowned for the quality of the beef on offer, The Westwood has become synonymous with superb quality meat. Although committed to sourcing local ingredients wherever possible, the beef for one of Matthew's signature dishes - the Casterbridge bone in rib-eye to share - comes from a little further a field, offering diners a taste of a truly great British product.

Casterbridge is a collective of farms in the Southwest of England, rearing traditional and rare breeds of British beef such as Aberdeen Angus, South Devon and Hereford. The beef is of the highest quality, and is hung for 28 days to mature giving a distinctive flavour and excellent texture, all of which add something extra special to the finished dish

SEARED SCOTTISH KING SCALLOPS, WITH BUTTERNUT SQUASH PURÉE, SAUTÉED WILD MUSHROOMS, SMOKED PANCETTA

SERVES 4

Ingredients

12 Scottish king scallops, cleaned and shelled, muscle and roe removed
50g girolle mushrooms
50g trompette de mort mushrooms
8 slices of pancetta

For the butternut squash purée

500g butternut squash, peeled, de-seeded and finely sliced
250g carrots, peeled and finely sliced
150ml whipping cream
70ml chicken stock
20g unsalted butter
1 shallot peeled and sliced
50g grated parmesan
1 clove of garlic
1 sprig of thyme
Salt

To garnish

Mustard cress
Black and white sesame seeds

Method

For the purée

Sweat the shallot, garlic, thyme and carrots in a heavy-bottomed pan with butter, cooking gently so the vegetables soften but do not colour.

Add the chicken stock and cook the carrots for 10 minutes or until tender. Add the butternut squash and whipping cream, and simmer for a further 8-10 minutes until the butternut squash has softened and broken down. Season with salt to taste.

Purée the vegetable mixture in a blender until smooth and pass through a fine sieve. Set aside.

For the mushrooms

Clean the mushrooms and sauté with a knob of butter until tender. Grill the pancetta until crisp set aside with the mushrooms and keep warm.

For the scallops

Finally lightly season then sear the scallops in a hot frying pan with a drizzle of olive oil for about 1 minute. Add a knob of unsalted butter to colour the scallops, flip them over and fry for a further minute then remove from the heat and sprinkle with sesame seeds.

To assemble

Warm the purée in a pan and divide between four plates. Place scallops on the purée, top with the pancetta, scatter wild mushrooms around the plate and garnish with mustard cress.

28/30ᵒᶻ CASTERBRIDGE BONE IN RIB-EYE STEAK, MARINATED IN MOLASSES, BOURBON AND THYME, WITH HORSERADISH CRÈME FRAICHÉ

SERVES 4

Ingredients

For the molasses marinade

175ml Molasses
3tbsp balsamic vinegar
2tbsp freshly cracked coarse black pepper
2 garlic gloves, crushed
5cm piece root ginger, peeled and grated
1tsp fresh thyme
1tsp dried chilli flakes
2tbsp sunflower oil
30ml bourbon
Salt and cracked black pepper
4 x 8oz rib-eye steak, matured for 21/28days
or one 30oz piece

A 30oz rib can be prepared by a good high street butcher, however the marinade works equally well with standard 8oz rib-eye steak.

For the horseradish crème fraîche

2tbsp horseradish
100ml crème fraîche
Small bunch of chives, finely chopped
Pinch of salt

Method

For the marinade

Gently heat the molasses over a medium heat with a little water to dissolve the sugar and create a syrup. Add the balsamic vinegar, black pepper, garlic, ginger, thyme and chilli flakes. Bring to a simmer, add the bourbon and sunflower oil then remove from the heat to cool. When the marinade has cooled, brush the beef with the marinade, and leave for a minimum of 2-3 hours or ideally overnight.

For the steak

Rub a griddle pan with olive oil and heat on the stove until very hot. For individual steaks, season the meat well and sear on both sides for 2 minutes then transfer to a preheated oven at 180°c and cook for a further 2–3 minutes. The result will be medium rare, so extend or reduce the cooking time if you prefer. (Cooking time for 30oz rib is approx 20 for medium rare at 200°c). Because of the high sugar content in the marinade the steaks will blacken slightly - don't worry as this adds to the flavour of the beef.

To assemble

In the restaurant the customers are served with a sauce plate which includes sauce béarnaise, red wine shallots with wild mushrooms, horseradish and chive crème fraîche and Roquefort and herb butter. Matthew's favourite is the horseradish crème – a delicious, easy to make option. Combine crème fraîche and good quality horseradish, season with salt and sprinkle the chopped chives on top.

WARM TREACLE TART, APPLE, BLACKBERRY & VICTORIA PLUM COMPOTE, PASSION FRUIT CURD

SERVES 12

Ingredients

For the pastry

500g flour
200g caster sugar
300g diced butter
1 whole egg
Zest of one lemon

For the filling

4 whole eggs
1 lemon, zest and juice
500ml golden syrup
400ml double cream
170g "panko" breadcrumbs (Japanese breadcrumbs)

Spiced apple, blackberry and plum compote

100ml red wine
50g caster sugar
1 cinnamon stick
2 star anise
6 Granny Smith apples
4 Victoria plums
2 punnets fresh blackberries

Passion fruit curd

5 large egg yolks
100g caster sugar
350ml of passion fruit juice
125g unsalted butter, cubed

Method

For the pastry and filling

Preheat oven to 180°c. Mix all dry ingredients in a food processor. Add the diced butter and mix until it resembles breadcrumbs. Mix in the egg until dough is formed. Chill in the fridge for 1 hour (steps 1-4 can be made the day before). Roll into non stick 9 inch tart case, 5mm in thickness, then place in the freezer. When frozen blind bake for 15 minutes with baking beans and parchment paper. Remove the beans and bake for a further 5 minutes. Drop the oven down to 160°c. For the filling whisk eggs and lemon zest and juice. Add cream and golden syrup, mix until smooth. Add the panko breadcrumbs. Bake for 30 minutes until golden. Serve warm with compote and passion fruit curd.

For the spiced apple, blackberry and plum compote

For the compote, in a large pan add the red wine, sugar and spices and reduce by half. Meanwhile prepare all the apples and plums in to 1 inch size pieces, add to the reduced syrup, simmer for 10 minutes until just tender. Remove from the heat, add the blackberries, cover with cling film and leave to rest.

For the passion fruit curd

Whisk yolks and sugar until pale and creamy. Whisk in passion fruit juice, cook over bain marie stirring all the time. When it starts to thicken, whisk in butter, cool, then serve.

148
WILLIAM
& VICTORIA

6 Cold Bath Road, Harrogate HG2 0NA

01423 521 510 (Restaurant) 01423 506 883 (Wine Bar)
www.williamandvictoria.com

William & Victoria restaurant and wine bar have been in the Straker family for over 25 years, serving traditional British cuisine in the heart of Harrogate.

William & Victoria's has developed a reputation for great food served in a relaxed and unfussy style, using locally sourced fresh ingredients.

"Will & Vics", as it is often fondly referred to, has earned the reputation for being a great Harrogate institution, popular with both locals and returning visitors to the beautiful Yorkshire Spa town.

The downstairs wine bar, with a fine stocked cellar, serves a range of traditional, simple, home cooked dishes that we probably ate as children, but now neither have the time or inclination to cook. Dishes such as the slow roast belly pork with crispy crackling and apple sauce or lamb Henry with mint and rosemary are firm favourites.

The upstairs restaurant is elegantly decorated with traditional high ceilings aimed to create the classic dining experience. The menu reflects the beautiful surrounding with it's fine tuned dishes that include William & Victoria's 'drunken bullock' or roast rack of Nidderdale lamb with an ever changing specials board that takes advantage of the fantastic local produce that Yorkshire has to offer.

David and Johanna Straker

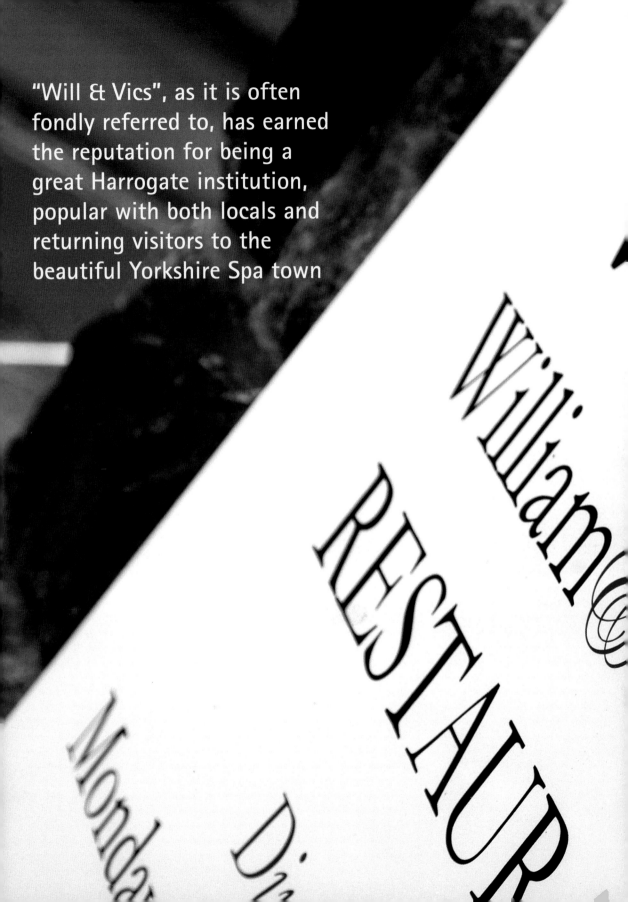

"Will & Vics", as it is often fondly referred to, has earned the reputation for being a great Harrogate institution, popular with both locals and returning visitors to the beautiful Yorkshire Spa town

PAN-FRIED CHICKEN LIVERS IN PINK PEPPERCORN SAUCE

SERVES 4

Ingredients

450g chicken livers
250ml double cream
2 shots of brandy (50ml)
Small handful of pink peppercorns
Salt and pepper
1 French baguette

Method

To start

Fry chicken livers on a medium heat until well sealed. Place under the grill until pink in the middle then return to the hob. Add the brandy and pink peppercorns and then flambé. Once all the alcohol has gone, add the double cream so the chicken livers are just covered and reduce to a thick creamy consistency and season.

To finish

To serve, slice and toast the French baguette and place the chicken livers on top.

WILLIAM & VICTORIA'S 'DRUNKEN BULLOCK'

SERVES 4

Ingredients

4x 225g (8oz) fillet steaks
4 baking potatoes
200g mushrooms
175ml red wine
250ml Guinness
50ml whisky
500ml double cream
500ml vegetable stock

Method

For the fondant potatoes

Peel the potatoes and place in a baking tray, cover with vegetable stock and bake in the oven for 40 minutes at 180°c.

For the sauce

Flambé the mushrooms with the whisky in a saucepan on a medium heat. Add the Guinness and the red wine, reduce by half then add the cream.

For the steak

Seal the steak in a hot pan with a small knob of butter. Transfer to a hot oven for 10 minutes (medium rare). Remove from oven and rest the steak for a few minutes before required.

Assembling the dish

To serve, place the steak on the fondant potato and smother with sauce.

STICKY TOFFEE PUDDING
TOFFEE SAUCE, ICE CREAM

SERVES 6

Method

For the pudding

Soak dates in boiling water for 5 minutes. While they are soaking, place the butter and sugar in a bowl and mix, then beat in the eggs, add the flour and fold in well. Drain the dates and add to mixture. Grease the cake tin and evenly spread the mixture. Place in the oven at 180°c for 35 minutes.

For the sauce

Place all the ingredients in a pan and bring to the boil. Put to one side ready for use.

To serve

Cut the sticky toffee pudding into even size portions, pour over some of the sauce and garnish with ice cream, if you wish.

Ingredients

Toffee pudding

225g chopped dates
1tsp bicarbonate of soda
125g butter
200g brown sugar
2 eggs
200g self-raising flour

Toffee Sauce

125g butter
175 double cream
200g brown sugar

CONTRIBUTORS

1885 THE RESTAURANT

The Recreation Ground, Stainland, Halifax,
West Yorkshire HX4 9HF

01422 373 030

www.1885therestaurant.co.uk

ARTISAN RESTAURANT

22 The Weir, Hessle, East Yorkshire HU13 0RU

01482 644 906

www.artisanrestaurant.com

THE BLUE BICYCLE

34 Fossgate York YO1 9TA

01904 673 990

www.thebluebicycle.com

THE BOX TREE

35–37 Church Street, Ilkley, West Yorkshire LS29 9DR

01943 608 484

www.theboxtree.co.uk

THE BURLINGTON RESTAURANT

The Devonshire Arms Country House Hotel and Spa,
Bolton Abbey, Near Skipton, North Yorkshire BD23 6AJ

01756 718 111

www.thedevonshirearms.co.uk

CLOCKTOWER

Rudding Park, Follifoot, Harrogate, North Yorkshire HG3 1JH

01423 871 350

www.ruddingpark.co.uk

THE FOURTH FLOOR AT HARVEY NICHOLS

107–111 Briggate, Leeds LS1 6AZ

0113 204 8000

www.harveynichols.com

THE GENERAL TARLETON INN

Boroughbridge Road, Ferrensby, Knaresborough HG5 0PZ

01423 340 284

www.generaltarleton.co.uk

HOTEL DU VIN AND BISTRO

Prospect Place, Harrogate HG1 1LB

01423 856 800

www.hotelduvin.com/harrogate

THE MAGPIE CAFÉ

14 Pier Road, Whitby, North Yorkshire YO21 3PU

01947 602 058

www.magpiecafe.co.uk

MIDDLETHORPE HALL & SPA

Bishopthorpe Road, York YO23 2GB

01904 641 241

www.middlethorpe.com

THE OLIVE TREE GREEK RESTAURANT

188-190 Harrogate Road, Chapel Allerton LS7 4NZ
01132 698 488

55 Rodley Lane, Rodley LS13 1NG
01132 569 283

74-76 Otley Road, Headingly LS6 4BA
01132 748 282

www.olivetreegreekrestaurant.co.uk

SAMUEL'S AT SWINTON PARK

Swinton Park, Masham, Ripon, North Yorks HG4 4JH

01765 680 900

www.swintonpark.com

THE WESTWOOD RESTAURANT

New Walk, Beverley, East Yorkshire HU17 7AE

01482 881 999

www.thewestwood.co.uk

WILLIAM & VICTORIA

6 Cold Bath Road, Harrogate HG2 0NA

01423 521 510 (Restaurant) 01423 506 883 (Wine Bar)

www.williamandvictoria.com

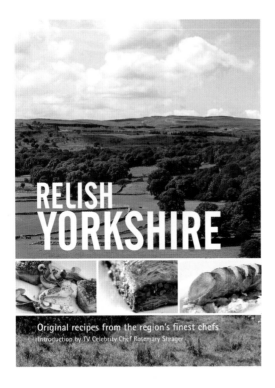

RELISH
YORKSHIRE

Original recipes from the region's finest chefs
Introduction by TV Celebrity Chef Rosemary Shrager

Good food is all about passion, creativity, taste
and experience. But it takes the talents of
enthusiastic and truly innovative chefs to bring it
to our attention – and make us want more.
Relish Yorkshire champions the very best
restaurants in this beautiful county, who offer
their own unique take on the freshest and best
local ingredients in recipes for you to create and
try at home.
There is much to celebrate. From fresh Whitby
crabs, Yorkshire rabbit, locally sourced lamb, not
to mention an abundance of fresh vegetables,
dairy produce and artisan gourmet products.
The magic ingredient, of course, is the talent of
chefs from this selection of fine–dining
restaurants and country house hotels.
All the chefs featured here have given away the
secrets of some of their signature dishes just for
you, so go on, create something delicious today.

For more information on
other books in this series
and to receive and share
recipes online please visit,
www.relishpublications.co.uk

RELISH
PUBLICATIONS.CO.UK